On the Way

40 DAYS TRAVELING WITH JESUS ON THE WAY TO THE CROSS

Kellye Jones

I dedicate this book to my Lord and Savior Jesus Christ. Thank you for taking me on this amazing journey.

To God our Creator.
Thank you for sending Your one and only Son into this world to save us and give us eternal life.

To my husband, Kevin Jones.
You are my biggest cheerleader. You are the one who encourages me to pursue my dream of writing.

To my children who are my honest editors.

Prologue

"Now on his way to Jerusalem, Jesus traveled along the border between Samaria and Galilee" Luke 17:11.

The text went out, "On the way." I was running late for a meeting with friends. I had a destination in mind and I wanted to convey a message that informed my friends I would be there soon, and I value their companionship.

My daughter sent out the same text just the other day. We were meeting for lunch. "On the way," the text read. I had picked up my mother and we were traveling down Mingo Street between Memorial and Garnett. Children were playing at the school playground. Cars were stopping and going at each intersection. The day was cooler than in the recent summer months, and I was enjoying this adventure until the reserve gas tank light blinked red. I stopped to fill up with gas because my mom did not want to live on the wild side. She did not want to hike anywhere to fetch a can of much needed fuel. We stopped and filled the car so that we could continue on to our destination. The journey to lunch was pleasant even though it was interrupted by plaguing blinking lights, but it wasn't as delightful as sitting at lunch with my daughter and mom.

"On the way." It's a simple text really, consisting of three short words a first grader can read. They are easy to type out and seem to be the universal text to let people know you are running late for a meeting. You have a specific destination and a specific time to be there. Three little words containing important information to inform people you are coming.

The scenery along the way may be pleasant, the weather comfortable, and you may enjoy watching all the people who cross your path. Your escapade may be fraught with unpleasant interruptions, but the journey is not the purpose of your travel. The final destination is your endgame.

We set out to our different destinations day by day, some days enjoying the ride other times not so much. We shift from one hip to the other during a twenty hour road trip. We get lost because we couldn't clarify the exits Google maps instructed us to take, and get confused as to how we landed at this intersection. The car behind us slams into our bumper because we have forgotten to signal for a left turn. The automobile shop informs us that our car is totaled because we forgot to use our rear view camera to see obstructions that lie behind us, or because we hit a patch of transparent ice and slide through the stop sign with oncoming traffic.

There are many roads chosen on this journey through life. The different roads we each take lead somewhere. We come upon varying intersections, and at times we may even meet one another at those intersections. Our vehicles glide by each other on freeways and toll roads. We bump along potholes, and have to pause to fill up with gas. The brakes of our cars squeal because we are riding them during traffic jams.

Life has become hard to navigate because of all the obstacles, but over two thousand years ago God sent a text of love into our world. "ON THE WAY." He sent us a Savior who came from heaven to earth to lead us as we travel. Because God so loved the world, He gave us His only Son to reroute us when we were lost. Jesus came to show us that He is the Way, the Truth, and the Life.

Our journey in this life will at times lead us into darkened and life threatening alleys, or tornadoes will rage around us, but Jesus commands us to journey onwards. He will be with us in the haunting alleys and fierce storms. He is our ship, our rudder and our Captain. He is the lighthouse that guides our paths.

Jesus traveled through this world "ON THE WAY" to his final destination. He walked through the countryside of Judea, Samaria, and Capernaum. A rugged hill outside of Jerusalem on a splintery cross was his fate. His end goal was an empty tomb carved into a rock slab. Jerusalem was the destination of Jesus' decisive confrontation with Satan.

"ON THE WAY" to that final destination, Jesus spent time with family. He was a good son to Mary and Joseph. According to Matthew 13:55-56, He was brother to men named James, Joseph, Judas, and Simon. He introduced himself to many new friends, and called a group of twelve to follow Him.

Jesus enjoyed the road trip. He stopped to party with tax collectors and outcasts. He paused to reach out and touch the lepers, the blind, and the lame. Jesus woke the dead from their sleep.

Though many loved and followed him throughout his travels, Jesus also became an enemy of the state. His words were radical and His philosophy was transforming. Romans and rulers of Israel alike were threatened by His teachings as Jesus traveled to a lonely, treacherous hill called Golgotha. The name means "the place of the skull." It was lined with Roman execution devices in the shape of the cross where they hung criminals and thieves. Though Jesus was neither, he joined the ranks of the condemned because God so loved the world He sent His Son to pay the ransom price for those who do not deserve it.

Family and friends lived His adventure from their side of history. They woke up each morning with the probability of seeing water turned into wine, or witnessing the heavens open up and hearing a voice say, "This is my beloved Son."

They lived a life worth living. They had no clue when they began the journey that they would see the blind receive sight, the deaf gain hearing, lepers become clean, and the dead raised to life. They followed Jesus of Nazareth from the courts of the Temple, through the hills of Judea and the water wells of Samaria. They knew, first hand, the love and compassion of Jesus because they witnessed it on a daily basis.

His enemies plotted and schemed at every step for various ways to derail Jesus' journey, yet He traveled onward. His face set like flint on that final destination. "Via Dolorasa" was the final road Jesus walked before His crucifixion. It was the road that led from Pontius Pilate's sentencing to Golgotha. Via Dolorasa literally meant the "Way of Sorrows." Jesus intimately knew the road of sorrow because He walked down it carrying a heavy wooden cross laden across his bloody back "ON THE WAY" to His final destination.

"ON THE WAY" through this life, we will also sail great distances. We will be tossed to and fro through many storms, but Jesus tells us not to fear the journey. He travels by our side. When we walk a trail of tears, remember Jesus has blazed this trail before us. He is our constant companion who has felt our every pain. It is not just sympathy He feels; it is empathy because He too has felt the lash of Satan's whip.

"Therefore, since we are surrounded by such a great cloud of witnesses, let us throw off everything that hinders and the sin that so easily entangles. And let us run with perseverance the race marked out for us, fixing our eyes on Jesus, the pioneer and perfector of our faith. For the joy set before him he endured the cross, scorning its shame and sat down at the right hand of the throne of God" Hebrews 12:1-2 NIV.

Join me "ON THE WAY" and follow Jesus from their side of His story. Don't pack any bags. You won't need them. All you need to follow Jesus is an open seeking heart, and He will give you the adventure of a lifetime, and a story that is worth telling to the world.

"Jesus told them, "Take nothing for the journey—no staff, no bag, no bread, no money, no extra shirt," Luke 9:3 NIV.

Lost and Found

Day One

"And the child grew and became strong in spirit, filled with wisdom; and the grace (favor and spiritual blessing) of God was upon Him," Luke 2:40 AMP.

"Every year Jesus' parents went to Jerusalem for the Passover festival. When Jesus was twelve years old, they attended the festival as usual. After the celebration was over, they started home to Nazareth, but Jesus stayed behind in Jerusalem.

His parents didn't miss him at first, because they assumed he was among the other travelers. But when he didn't show up that evening, they started looking for him among their relatives and friends. When they couldn't find him, they went back to Jerusalem to search for him there. Three days later they finally discovered him in the Temple, sitting among the religious teachers, listening to them and asking questions. All who heard him were amazed at his understanding and his answers. His parents didn't know what to think.

"Son," his mother said to him, "why have you done this to us? Your father and I have been frantic, searching for you everywhere." "But why did you need to search?" he asked. "Didn't you know that I must be in my Father's house?" But they didn't understand what he meant." Luke 2:41-50 NLT.

The definition of lost is "to become unable to find something or someone." Mary and Joseph had lost the Son of

God. They began their journey home unaware they had misplaced a priceless treasure. How would you like to begin a journey lost? I do that quite often as I come out of malls or grocery stores. I forget where I parked my car. I know you know what that feels like. I can't be the only one. I live in a lost state most days. I forget where I put my shoes. I misplace my keys. Lost is a four letter word that has become my mantra. I have even lost or misplaced my own children just like Mary and Joseph.

When Landry was seven, we had a Sunday morning routine. We liked to go to early service at 8:00, then at 9:30 we would separate and each family member would go to their respective Sunday School classes. There was also an 11:00 service, but we rarely went to that one. However, this certain Sunday we changed it up. Kevin and I had taken separate cars to church because he had an early meeting that Sunday morning. The kids and I weren't ready so we opted for the second schedule. I took each child to their class and I met Kevin in our Sunday school. At 11:00 we met at worship as a family unit. When the service ended, we decided on our Sunday restaurant. "Okay, meet you there." Each parent assumed the kids would follow one of us out the door. Don't ever assume your child will naturally follow you like a mother duck and her ducklings.

I met Kevin at the restaurant. "Where's Landry?" I asked joining Kevin at the table with Nikki and Magen following close behind me. "I thought he was with you," Kevin said, a small amount of alarm rising in his voice.

"I thought he was with you," my voice nearing hysteria. "You stay here with the girls. I'll go back to church," Kevin informed me calmly. Kevin was always the one who could stay cool in the midst of frenzy, but I know he drove at least

80 going down the streets of Artesia. We had misplaced our son at church and we had to find him. Kevin was my guy for that mission.

"Found him," Kevin told me over the phone. "He thought he was suppose to go to Sunday School after church. He fell asleep in his class because the lights were off." I breathed a sigh of relief. "Thank you God." I didn't know at the time that I would one day use this as an illustration for this book.

I identify with Mary and Joseph. I have felt Mary's panic before. I only wish that were the only time I misplaced a child. I have had that lost child panic syndrome on multiple occasions. It's the realization that you don't know where your three year old son is, only to find him hiding in the middle of the rack of clothing while shopping at the mall. Or, you turn around and realize your eight year old daughter isn't with your group as you travel through Six Flags. You panic just as Mary did.

"Son," his Mother said to him, "why have you done this to us? Your father and I have been frantic, searching for you everywhere." As a parent you go from euphoria because you have located your child to being angry that they got away from your side. I identify with Mary's reaction as she and Joseph found Jesus. She was distraught with fear.

Twelve year old Jesus simply replied, "But why did you need to search?" Didn't you know that I must be in my Father's house?" It was Jesus' first recorded words in scripture. They were offered simply, not as an excuse, but as an inquiry. With this reply Jesus states His mission for all His life here on earth. He knew who He was and where He had come from and what He must be about doing.

Mary and Joseph were unable to find Jesus among the places they assumed He should have been, thus, this fit their definition of lost. Upon finding Him Jesus explained to them that He was not lost because He had never moved. He had stayed in the same place they had last seen Him. It was they who lost sight of Him.

I have heard the excuses, "But mommy I was just playing," or "Mommy, I turned around and you weren't there." Those excuses don't ease the pit in your stomach because of the panic of losing a child, but how can you argue with Jesus, the Son of God? He knew who He was and He knew who His Father was. He had to be in His Father's house.

Jesus called God, "Abba." It is a term of endearment. It means dear Father. On this day, at this time Jesus knew this was what He must do. He must be about His Father's business.

Joseph and Mary found Jesus discussing the spiritual philosophies with some of the greatest Jewish minds of the day. This was His order of business for this day. These men were known as master teachers, professors, doctors, lawyers and Pharisees. Jesus was marveling them with a wisdom that was otherworldly. This juvenile discussed deep religious matters with the most learned and wisest of the biblical scholars of his day. The bible says of Jesus, "listening to them and asking questions." "All who heard Him were amazed at His understanding and His answers." Jesus astonished these great spiritual minds. The Greek word for astonished is existemi. It literally means to astonish out of their wits. I wonder, did they stare at Him stupefied? Were their mouths gaping? His questions stirred them to reach deep into their knowledge. His answers made them scratch their heads.

Jesus was and is the Son of the Ancient of Days. Jesus has been there from before time began. Through Him all things were created. Jesus wrote the book these scholars studied, and wrote the script to the play they were enacting. He had designed this set. They were sitting in the very Temple He created. He was in the director's seat guiding each character. They thought they knew it all, and they had this life journey figured out. However, they were at a complete loss to explain how this 12 year old boy contained such wisdom. It was a wisdom as old as time itself, and came from deep in His soul because He had been around before the beginning. Jesus was a year away from celebrating His Bar Mitzvah. In one year He would be held accountable and would be responsible to observe the commandments of God. He was light years ahead of that schedule.

Jesus did have it all figured out because He knew the whole story of man. He was the one who authored our story. He knew perfectly and completely all of the facts of life. He replied and answered these scholars from His depth of knowledge that was sourced from His Father Abba in heaven. Jesus had been with the Creator before time began.

Oh to have been a fly on the Temple wall watching wisdom and knowledge volleying back and forth from youth to scholar. I smirk as I think of each of these brilliant minds trying to teach the beautiful mind of Jesus. He had all their answers. They couldn't stump Him with their theology. It was Philosophy 101 and He became the professor.

I took Philosophy 101 in college. I dropped it the next day. It was too taxing on my 18 year old mind. I just wasn't into all that rhetoric. Sometimes I think professors talk to impress themselves. Jesus wasn't about to drop this philosophy class. These professors may have been talking to hear their own voices but Jesus left them with their jaws dropping. His words were truth. His questions were stimulating and He exited with them wanting more.

He returned to the Temple each year because his parents were faithful and adhered to the Law of Moses. Every year Jesus would worship in His Father's House with His earthly family. The Rabbi's would read from the Torah and teach the pilgrims of the mighty deliverance of God as the nation of Israel escaped from the evil hand of Pharaoh. Jesus would sit in the Temple courts and listen to stories that He authored.

That is my Rabboni! That's my great teacher! I am sitting in His class "Life 101." Jesus is my Professor. I trust His philosophy because His is a wisdom born from The Ancient of Days.

Jesus is the same yesterday, today and tomorrow. His wisdom has not diminished, and He has not moved. He is still at the right-hand of the Throne of God. It is us who have lost sight of Jesus. Like Mary and Joseph we have let clouds of busyness, anxiety, depression, and fear obscure our view of Jesus. We need to do what Mary and Joseph did. Retrace our steps and return to the place where we left Him. When we find Him we will find a treasure chest of wisdom.

The Place Where Wisdom Begins

She and Joseph had been frantic for the past three days. They had left Jerusalem a day ago. She knew where most of her children were. It had been hard to keep up with her large crew. Most of her and Joseph's family traveled together to make the pilgrimage from Nazareth to Jerusalem. It was one hundred and forty miles. It had been a hard and exerting trek. They had traveled five days to get to the Passover feast. Now, they were one day into the return trip. Mary would ring the dinner bell and get her husband and children fed and put to bed for another long hike tomorrow.

One by one they came filing in. They were hungry and tired from traipsing up and down the rocky hills. The family unit gathered to say a blessing over the food.

Where was Jesus? Mary went to her parent's campsite. Joseph searched among his kinfolk. They came back together wide eyed and hearts gathering in their throats. He wasn't among their caravan.

They had lost The Son of God. It was their responsibility to take care of Him, their life's purpose and they had failed.

Mary and Joseph flew out of the encampment. They retraced their steps and arrived back in Jerusalem. It was the beginning place of this entire nightmare. Running up the Temple steps and breathless, they flew into the Temple courts, and heard the voices of the scholars and teachers of the law. They also heard His voice. It was the sound of that cherished voice, the voice of their son, the voice of God, and it was paradise to their ears.

The knot in the pit of their stomach eased. They had found Him. Anger and bewilderment replaced their fear over losing a child. Jesus would get a good scolding before this day ended to be sure. How could he cause them such anxiety?

They paused momentarily to observe the scene laid out before them. A group of scholarly professors surrounded their Son. The scene was just short of comical watching these professors with mouths gaping because of the words, questions, and answers that poured from this mild-mannered inquisitive twelve year old boy.

Jesus sat respectfully as He listened to their questions, "Yes sir, I understand," He would respond. Showing each teacher the honor they deserved. Each teacher would lean forward as He spoke, hanging onto His answers.

Mary and Joseph rushed in and stood before Him. Mary grasped him by the shoulders. She needed to physically touch this Child she had lost. "Son, why have you treated us like this? Your father and I have been anxiously searching for you," Luke 2:48 NIV. Jesus never ceased to amaze her as He answered her matter of fact. "Why were you searching for Me?" he asked. "Didn't you know I had to be in my Father's house," Luke 2:49 NIV.

Mary had no comeback. She looked into Jesus' eyes and saw a wisdom that flowed from an everlasting past. She and Joseph had never taught Him these things. These answers flowed from the Father above.

Mary collected herself; Joseph shrugged. This child had upended her life once again. An aura of mystery encircled the trio. Simeon's words flooded her thoughts, "A sword will pierce your own soul." It had begun. The sharp pain of love stabbed her heart as she took Jesus into her arms.

He was crossing the threshold of becoming a man. Mary began to lose her child, but somehow she knew she had gained a Savior. She tucked the memory into her treasure chest of memories. It was where wisdom flowed.

On the Way

Waypoints to your destination:

Have you ever felt that panic that Mary described?

What do you think of Jesus' words, "Didn't you know I had to be in my Father's house?"

What does verse 46 say that Jesus was doing when Mary and Joseph found him?

What was the effect Jesus had on the scholars of the day?

"Lord open my mind and thoughts to Your wisdom. You know everything. You know my past, my present and my future. Open up my wonder to Your Amazing Grace."

Home Sweet Home

Day Two

"Then he went down to Nazareth with them and was obedient to them. But his mother treasured all these things in her heart. And Jesus grew in wisdom and stature, and in favor with God and man" Luke 2:51-52 NIV.

I wonder, did Mary ever have to turn away from Jesus' insightful gaze? I can't even imagine how intimidating it must have been to be the parents of the only sinless child who ever walked the face of this earth. How would you have liked to have been one of Jesus' siblings? My mind can't even go there. I am just trying to wrap my head around raising a perfect child, and to top it off, a perfect boy.

Mary never had to run after Him because He broke away from her grasp and darted in front of a donkey cart. Mary never got a crick in her neck because she tried to pick Jesus up to lead him in her direction while He pulled away so that He could go in the direction of His choosing. Mary never had to persuade Jesus to share because Jesus never had a selfish moment in his life.

Mary and Joseph, and His siblings often displayed their selfishness. They had to have because the bible says, "For all have sinned and come short of the glory of God;" Romans 3:23 KJV.

Mary and Joseph needed a Savior the same as you and me, but they were raising the Savior of the world. Did Mary or Joseph's sins and shortcomings stick out like a sore

10

thumb up against Jesus' spotless ways? I get a little anxious thinking about that. I remember my shortcomings as I tried to be a good parent. I made my fair share of mistakes, but so did my children, and so did my husband. We were all in this sin thing together. Mary and Joseph and Jesus' siblings were out on the limb alone as Jesus grew in wisdom and stature, and in favor with God and man. He who was sinless was raised in a family of sinners. God's grace definitely had to fill in on this lopsided family dynamic.

Twelve year old Jesus, Son of God, went home with his earthly parents and submitted to their authority in His life. Verse 52 tells us that day in and day out, Jesus increased in wisdom and stature. The wisdom He gained matured His thought process. His Papa Abba, His Heavenly Father grew prouder and prouder of His Son and the life He was living on this earth, until one day God would open up the sky and His Holy Spirit would descend on Jesus like a dove, and God would speak from heaven, "You are my dearly loved Son, and you bring me great joy." Talk about speaking identity into someone.

Jesus became strong in spirit. Jesus' strength came from His Father in heaven. It was a dominating strength from a heavenly source. As I write those words I am singing Bonnie Tyler's song, "I need a hero." Everyone needs a hero. Jesus is mine. We all need a Savior. We all need someone who is bigger than our wrong-doings. Mary and Joseph needed a hero and He was living right under their noses. The One they were raising had more wisdom in a single thought than the sum total of each of their thoughts. He was complete wisdom. His was a perfected wisdom because He had come from God. His wisdom came because He is The Ancient of Days.

Mary treasured and wrote all these things in her heart. I am so thankful she did. She held passionately to these events. Not a moment of those days slipped from her memory. Mary knew that underneath her roof lay the Son of God, the Son of Man. She never had to discipline Jesus because He was sent to discipline her and guide her back to a right relationship with her Father in heaven.

That's my Son

The LORD God, Creator of heaven and earth, couldn't help but smile as He watched His Son grow and thrive upon the earth. The smile went from ear to ear, and was an outpouring of the great depth of love He held for His One and Only Son. In the dimension of time and space, His child was just a young lad playing upon the earth. Jesus had not yet reached the age of manhood, but Father God, kept an ever watchful eye gazing toward His Son. Theirs was a love no word could describe. It was born because Father and Son were eternally entwined.

His Son had gone sacrificially into the world. Jesus willingly left His Father's side. He entered their world as an innocent baby, but was now growing as a juvenile in their culture. Father God swelled with pride as He observed Jesus continually submitting to the authority of Joseph and Mary. Such respect He displayed before them as their son. Jesus contained no selfish bones inside Him. He embodied the nature of sacrifice. He would give all to serve the people He came to save.

Both Father and Son felt the great love for the humans they had created. The creatures needed a Savior, and because He was the perfect Son of God, He went.

Jesus submitted to their laws of nature. He grew in the ways of children, from child to juvenile, but He steered clear of the selfish ways of man. He grew and increased in wisdom. His strength and stature among his peers was noticeable. He could win any race but humbly submitted to his friends because a friend loves at all times. He wanted what was best for each childhood friend. He could have lorded over His brothers, James, Joseph, Jude, and Simon, yet he didn't. He washed their feet and tended to their cuts and bruises. That was His nature. He was servant and healer all wrapped into one, and He grew in favor of God, family, and friends.

He lived to ever please His Father in heaven, and pleased God was. "That's my Son," He spoke as He applauded from heaven.

Waypoints to your destination:

What do you think it was like raising the sinless Son of God?

What did Jesus increase in?

What do you think it might have been like to carry on a conversation with Jesus?

What did God think of His Son at this time?

"Lord, may I treasure You above all else. Fill my heart with the love of the Father. May I love You with the love of God."

Where the Wild Things Are

Day Three

The word of God came to John son of Zechariah in the wilderness. He went into all the country around the Jordan, preaching a baptism of repentance for the forgiveness of sins. As it is written in the book of the words of Isaiah the prophet: "A voice of one calling in the wilderness, 'Prepare the way for the Lord, make straight paths for him. Every valley shall be filled in, every mountain and hill made low. The crooked roads shall become straight, the rough ways smooth. And all people will see God's salvation.'" Luke 3:1-6 NIV.

Each of my grandsons have loved the book, "Where the Wild Things Are." Ezekiel however, at age thirteen months, has begun to act out the book. Whenever he hears the words, "Let the wild rumpus start," Zekey gnashes his terrible teeth, raises his terrible claws, and roars his terrible roar. Then he begins to stomp his feet in a wild rumpus around the coffee table and Zeke becomes a wild thing.

Around 27 A.D., there rose up another type of wildling out of the wilderness of Judea. The first four letters of wilderness form the word "wild," and it was in this type of terrain that the Word of God came to a man called John the Baptist. He was an organic mountain man. His look characterized the wilderness around him. His clothes were made from camel hair with a leather belly bag cinched around his waist. For food he ate locusts and wild honey. John was an intimidating person who felt more at home in the great

15

outdoors than in the formal dining rooms of the Jewish hierarchy.

God did not call a man with formal learning or who had attended rabbinical Torah schools. God had a job for John of the wilderness. He spoke to John in the place where the wild things are. John had fire in his gut. He was the pioneer of "Man vs Wild." He would have stuck out like a sore thumb on the streets of Manhattan. John's thunderous voice boomed across the shores and rippled across the waters of the river. "Wake up and get your heart ready for the coming of the Lord Jesus!"

The southeast corner of New Mexico can be labeled one of the driest parts of the United States. I know. I grew up there, and I raised my children there. As a little girl I would go out with my dad to the oil patch east of town and try to dig up a piece of the dried earth that had cracked like jigsaw puzzle pieces because of the desert heat.

The White Sands of New Mexico were just a couple of hours away. White sand dunes spread to the horizon without a patch of vegetation. Mom and dad would take my brother and me on outings and picnics to these white hills. I remember climbing to the top of a sand dune and rolling down hill, but it wasn't a place to visit during the heat of summer months. The sand would scorch your feet. It was the desert after all.

The desert, the wastelands, and the wilderness are not the most exciting of places. There are no sandy beaches or rolling ocean waves to come and break into your horizon. For as far as you can see there is nothing but barrenness in a desert. Then there is the wilderness, where utter chaos seems to abound in this world that God created. Brambles and thorn bushes aplenty reach out to scrape and bruise your knees and block your paths. My husband is addicted to the National

Geographic channel. Documentaries on the wastelands where lions and tigers fight for water rights are his favorite. They feature the rhinoceros and the hippos bathing in mud swamps, soaking in the last drop of water that once filled an oasis. It's a wild landscape. It is where the wild things are and at times many of us have been there.

In a separate desert in a different time, God spoke to another man named Moses. God's word came from a burning bush while Moses was a desert dweller. "Now Moses was tending the flock of Jethro his father-in-law, the priest of Midian. And he led the flock to the back of the desert, and came to Horeb, the mountain of God. And the Angel of the LORD appeared to him in a flame of fire from the midst of a bush. So he looked and behold, the bush was burning with fire, but the bush was not consumed" Exodus 3:1-2 NIV. "When the Lord saw that he had gone over to look, God called to him from within the bush, "Moses! Moses!" Exodus 3:4 NIV.

Moses was on the backside of the desert. God still found him even there at the furthest point of this barren place. The definition of a desert is a desolate or forbidding area devoid of life and water supply. Moses was at the deepest point of this desolate land and still God called him from there.

Another great man of God, the prophet Isaiah, felt as if he were in a wasteland after his beloved King Uzziah had died, but even in the wasteland God revealed Himself to His faithful prophet. "In the year that King Uzziah died, I saw the Lord sitting on a throne, high and lifted up, the train of His robe filled the temple" Isaiah 6:1 NIV. Uzziah's reign was a good reign in the eyes of the Lord. It is said of Uzziah, "And he did what was right in the sight of the LORD, according to all that his father Amaziah had done" 2 Chronicles 26:3 NIV.

At the time Isaiah saw the Lord sitting on a throne, high and lifted up, Isaiah would have been mourning the death of a great king, as all Israel would have been. Isaiah's head would have been downcast because Israel just lost a king who worshipped the Lord and had led Israel to worship the Great I Am.

I think back to the year JFK was assassinated and the great shock and mourning that went throughout this country. That was the spirit of Israel at the death of King Uzziah. God revealed himself to Isaiah during his time of great loss. It was at this point God ushered Isaiah into his higher calling.

Desert places, dry places, wilderness places, wastelands and places of mourning, they are both physical and spiritual. They are the landscapes where you feel devoid of life. They are lonely desolate places, but these can also be our preparation places. I have called them wastelands before, but I am learning that nothing is wasted in God's Kingdom. We may feel as if we are on the very backside of the desert, but God can find us anywhere. God can use us in the dry barren places and God leads us through our wildernesses. He carries us as we travel the wastelands, and our badlands are not out of His reach.

Why is this? Why do we have to travel through the deserts, the wildernesses, the wastelands, and the badlands? Is it because sometimes that is the only place God can get our attention? Maybe that is the only place God can shut out all the noise of the world so that you can hear His instruction. I don't know. All I know is, "the word of God came to John, son of Zechariah, in the desert."

I have felt that dry barren place deep in my soul. It happens every season I neglect God's Word. I become as dry as the parched desert ground when it cracks like puzzle pieces. I have also witnessed the rains of heaven pouring down, filling those cracks in the dirt. That rain is my reminder to return and open up my bible that is covered in dust. The word of God becomes my bottle of water as I wander alone and parched through my desert place.

The Wild One

Tiberius Caesar walked the palace steps. The opulent window veils floated with the breeze. It was now the fifteenth year of his reign. He was enjoying the calmness that surrounded him. Tiberius did not see or sense the storm brewing on the horizon of his realm. He had sent Pontius Pilate to Judea to become governor of the region. He hoped Pilate had the wisdom and the wherewithal to maintain peace in Judea. Herod the tetrarch of Galilee was a hothead and was full of himself. Surely Pilate could contain and reel this windbag in. Annas and Caiaphas were the high priests of the strange Jewish religion that dominated throughout Judea. These two were a constant friction to the peace Tiberius wanted to establish in the southern region of his Roman kingdom. Peace reigned but it was precarious at best, always teetering at the edge of the cliff.

There was another man as different in mannerism as night was to day. John did not walk in the halls of a royal palace. He walked in the outdoors of God's creation. He loved this wild place that was devoid of any semblance of organization. For some reason this was the place he called home. It was his comfortable place. He had left the home of his father and mother because for an unknown reason he felt the call of the wild. Once he had arrived in this arid region of Judea, he knew this was the place he was to be for this season in his life. The call of El Elyon, the Most High God, had led him to this barren place, so here he would stay and await his next step. "A voice of one calling in the desert...."

John knew the miraculous events that surrounded his birth. His parents, Elizabeth and Zechariah, had described each one, and retold them to John throughout his life. Every year on his birthday, his father reminded him, "And you, child, will be called the prophet of the Highest; For you will go before the face of the Lord to prepare His ways, to give knowledge of salvation to His people by the remission of their sins." John loved and respected his father. Zechariah had spoken life and purpose into him. John knew who he was, and knew what he was appointed to do. He just didn't know when.

John dug beneath the rock to find the locust crawling beneath. He plucked it up and popped the bug into his mouth. It was covered with the sticky wild honey from John's fingertips. The beehive hung low from the branch. John was careful not to get stung. He had waited for the bees to swarm around the wildflowers on the floor of the wilderness before he reached in to taste the succulent honey. "John," he heard a voice call out to him in the breeze blowing through the wilderness. "John, it is time to go. I led you to the wilderness to teach you diligence, but that time has passed. Prepare the way for My Son. Make straight the crooked roads for Him. Fill in every valley. Level the mountain and the hill. Smooth out the rough places. Throw out the rocks and boulders. The wilderness was the beginning point of your journey, but now the Lord your God is calling you out of the wild."

John was prepared. The words of his father rang through his memory. His voice roared loud and clear to the people of Judea, "Repent, for the kingdom of heaven has come near. I baptize you with water. But one who is more powerful than I will come, the straps of whose sandals I am not worthy to untie.

He will baptize you with the Holy Spirit and fire" Luke 3:16-17 NIV.

Waypoints to your destination:

Do you feel like you are in a desert place?

Where did John hear the Word of the Lord?

What season was Isaiah in when he saw the Lord high and lifted up?

What can you do to get your eyes off the barren wastelands and onto the Lord?

"Lord as I travel through the barren places, help me to focus on You. You are Living Water. You are an oasis in the desert. Help me keep my eyes on You."

Down by the River

Day Four

"I baptize with water," John replied, "but among you stands one you do not know. He is the one who comes after me, the straps of whose sandals I am not worthy to untie" John 1:26-27 NIV.

"This all happened at Bethany on the other side of the Jordan, where John was baptizing. The next day John saw Jesus coming toward him and said, "Look, the Lamb of God who takes away the sin of the world!" John 1:28-29 NIV.

"Then Jesus came from Galilee to the Jordan to be baptized by John. But John tried to deter Him, saying, 'I need to be baptized by you and do you come to me?" Jesus replied, 'Let it be so now; it is proper for us to do this to fulfill all righteousness" Matthew 3:13-15 NIV.

"As soon as Jesus was baptized, He went up out of the water. At that moment heaven was opened, and He saw the Spirit of God descending like a dove and alighting on Him. And a voice from heaven said, 'This is my Son, whom I love: with Him I am well pleased" Matthew 3:16-17 NIV.

One of my favorite TV reality shows is the "Amazing Race." Contestants fly across the globe experiencing the cultures of the nations. I think I might enjoy the contest, but none of my family members are willing to join my team. I think it is because they know it would be them who had to carry the brunt of the burden to complete the race. I do not eat bugs or other gross stuff. I don't like the heat. I will need a blanket in the cold, and I like the finer five star hotels. Sleeping in airports or under the stars is a little too offensive for my delicate skin, but I am good at reading maps because I have stayed in a Holiday Inn. My family will not choose me, but Jesus has chosen me to tag along as He went on His "Amazing Race."

The son of Mary and Joseph was now a grown man. It was 30 A.D. Jesus had a destiny and a purpose to walk in. He heard the sound of His Father's starting gun, and He was off on His amazing race. Jesus left his childhood home in Nazareth, and traveled to the shores of the Jordan River. This was the Father's starting leg of His journey to the cross. He had a divine appointment on this day. He was to meet his cousin John the Baptist.

John had proven he was passionate for the things of God, and because he had the right heart condition, he experienced a Holy Moment with His Savior.

The setting of Jesus' first public encounter was on the shore of the Jordan River. He walked intentionally toward John. He knew His next step. He had to be lowered into the swirling waters of the Jordan River. His cousin was to be His baptizer. Jesus, the Lamb of God who takes away the sin of the world, needed to be washed by the waters that He had created.

Jesus and John the Baptist were as different as any two you know. Each was called to run different races. John had a booming voice beckoning all to repentance, and Jesus exhibited His own disposition of grace and mercy. John was used to prepare the way for Jesus. Jesus came to bear the cross and defeat death, hell, and the grave for a dying world.

An unlikely pair, but each ran their God-appointed races and ran them well.

"For John the Baptist came neither eating bread nor drinking wine, and you say, 'He has a demon.' The Son of Man has come eating and drinking, and you say, 'Here is a glutton and a drunkard, a friend of tax collectors and sinners'" Luke 7:33-34 NIV.

I gasped as I watched the American women's four by one hundred meter relay team drop the baton during the exchange between Alyson Felix and English Gardner during the 2016 Olympics. The team was poised to win it all; instead the dropped baton disqualified them. With quick thinking Felix urged Gardner to pick up the baton and finish the race. If they were to have a chance at repealing the disqualification, Gardner had to cross the finish line. The women won their appeal and ran another qualifying relay all by themselves the next morning. They came in with the leading time of 41.77 seconds. That night the U.S. Women's 4x100 meter relay team claimed their coveted dream. They won gold with a time of 41.01 seconds.

The original ruling of disqualification came because Allyson Felix was bumped by a Brazilian runner in the next lane. Felix's stride was thrown off balance causing the exchange to be faulty. The baton was dropped and Felix picked it up and threw it to Gardner who finished the ill fated race.

God has called each of us to run His amazing race. He doesn't call us to run every race. Those who are meant to run the sprints, God empowers to run sprints. Others are called to run relays and others marathons. We have but one race, and all God asks is to run it well and cross the finish line.

Our Coach instructs us to stay in the lane He has designed for us. The people in the next lane may bump us and throw us off balance. Our batons may drop, but God says, "Finish the race. I will be with you wherever you go." Our race may not look pretty and it might not even be the one we've dreamed of winning, but when we cross that final finish line we will hear the words, "Well done, good and faithful servant."

The Amazing Race

John woke up that morning and wiped the dust off his camel hair robe. His bones were weary and his muscles ached. He must have dunked hundreds of people in the Jordan River over the past few days. He didn't mind though; the aches and pains reminded him of the fight he was engaged in. He had been given an assignment from God. That assignment had been poured into him from before he was even conceived. He knew his lane and he was running in it all the way to the finish line.

During those days, everyone was gripped with messianic expectations. They believed the Messiah would come at any moment. They flocked to the Jordan to be baptized by John. John spoke the message of repentance, and it sliced though the listener's very souls and pierced their hearts.

It was time. It was past time for the children of Abraham to get their hearts right before the Lord, so that is what he preached. John told the crowds, "I baptize only with water." So he walked out into the Jordan and began the dunking, symbolically washing each one who desired repentance, but in his heart he knew there would be One who would baptize in the power of the Holy Spirit. Day after day he too longed to see the One who would come after him whose sandals he was not worthy to untie.

Jesus put on the outer robe his mother, Mary, had woven for Him. He kissed her cheek and tasted the tear rolling down. He could see the plea written in the sorrow of her eyes. "Don't go," He knew she wanted to beg, but He also knew she would never say it. She felt the winds of change blowing the same as He did. The words of Gabriel echoed down the halls of time.

Jesus felt the fear and dread that shrouded their good-byes. It was a fear that was evident in her shallow breaths. Jesus knew Simeon's words spoken to her thirty years ago engulfed her heart. "A sword will pierce your own soul."

Mary's nails dug into His shoulders as she kissed Him, then she released her son. They said their good-bye's. He felt her penetrating gaze follow Him down the lane as He walked into the world He had created with His Father.

His Amazing Race had begun. The Father had revealed it to Him. He descended the hills of Nazareth. He had an appointment at the Jordan River. His Father had made it. He knew who He must meet, He knew where they must meet, and He knew what the meeting would accomplish. His Father in Heaven was sending Him. His Father had prepared Him. He too had been given an assignment, but there was one thing He must accomplish before He was propelled to run the race.

He walked the 30 miles and found His cousin baptizing in the Jordan River, right where His Father had sent Him. He walked into the River and clasped the hand of His cousin in greeting. They had met before. They had met in each of their mother's wombs before either had even been born into this world. John recognized Jesus then with excitement, and he recognized Jesus now with humility.

"I will be baptized by you, John, on this very day," Jesus said to the Baptizer. "I need to be baptized by you, and do you come to me?" John spoke humbly to His Messiah. "Let it be so now; it is

proper for us to do this to fulfill all righteousness." Both Savior and servant had a desire to do everything right before God Most High.

John took the Savior of the world, the Lamb of God, his Cousin, into His arms and immersed Jesus into the flowing water of the Jordan River. His heart pounded because this was a Holy Moment and he was thankful the Lord allowed him to be a part of it.

Jesus came up praying as His face broke the plane of the water. His eyes were cast to the skies. He and John both saw the heavens open. Then Jesus saw His Heavenly Father release the Holy Spirit of God. God's Spirit descended like a dove and lit upon His shoulder. He remembered the dove Noah had released once a long time ago. Noah never knew where the dove landed but Jesus always had His eye on that dove, and now the Spirit of God had come to Him in that form.

Jesus heard His Father's booming voice once again, "This is my Son whom I love; with Him I am well pleased." That voice and those words gave Him courage. With the knowledge that His Father was pleased with Him, He could face the challenges and the wildernesses of this earth. And He walked off to run His Race.

Waypoints to your destination:

What was John doing on this day?

How did John describe Jesus as He walked toward him?

What was John's attitude when Jesus told John to baptize Him?

What did God say as Jesus rose from the waters?

"Lord, may I decrease as You increase. Lord, may I walk in the purpose You have called me to. Help me to run my race for the glory of God."

Finding Yourself

Day Five

"At that time Jesus came from Nazareth in Galilee and was baptized by John in the Jordan. Just as Jesus was coming up out of the water, He saw heaven being torn open and the Spirit descending on Him like a dove. And a voice came from heaven: "You are my Son, whom I love; with you I am well pleased." At once the Spirit sent him out into the wilderness, and he was in the wilderness forty days, being tempted by Satan. He was with the wild animals, and angels attended him" Mark 1:9-13 NIV.

"The next day John saw Jesus coming toward him and said, "Look, the Lamb of God, who takes away the sin of the world! This is the one I meant when I said, 'A man who comes after me has surpassed me because He was before me.' I myself did not know Him, but the reason I came baptizing with water was that He might be revealed to Israel." Then John gave this testimony: "I saw the Spirit come down from heaven as a dove and remain on Him. And I myself did not know Him, but the one who sent me to baptize with water told me, 'The man on whom you see the Spirit come down and remain is the one who will baptize with the Holy Spirit.' I have seen and I testify that this is God's Chosen One" John 1:29-34NIV.

Many people in our lives are suffering an identity crisis. The high school star athlete who goes to college and suddenly nobody knows his name; the busy mom who now has a quiet house because of her empty nest; or the oilfield worker who lost his job because the price of oil has dipped so low his company can no longer afford to keep him on; and the list goes on. It is long and distinguished.

I have suffered an identity crisis a time or two in my own life. You begin to feel like you are free falling through your days. I know my cure for my identity crisis though. I must know who I am in Christ!

Webster defines crisis as a time of intense difficulty, trouble, or danger.

Synonyms of crisis include emergency, disaster, catastrophe, and calamity. It is a time when a difficult or important decision must be made. A time of crisis is a critical point. It is the time when things must turn around or you can't go on. You are at a point of no return. When we reach our zero hour, we must know who God says we are.

Jesus got His affirmation in the middle of the flowing waters of the Jordan River. His identity was confirmed, not by man, but by His Father in heaven. What a sight it must have been as Jesus came up out of the Jordan River on that day! Imagine seeing the heavens open up and hearing the thunderous voice of God as He proclaimed His love for His Son, Jesus. "After Jesus was baptized, He came up immediately out of the water; and behold, the heavens were opened, and he (John) saw the Spirit of God descending as a dove and lighting on Him (Jesus)" Matthew 3:16 AMP. The public display of affection was tangible. It was a physical manifestation of the Holy Spirit of God affirming His Son. John saw it with his own two eyes.

Each of the gospel writers recorded this event. They must have interviewed the eyewitnesses who had stood on the shores of the Jordan that day. Before his beheading, John the Baptist had to have shared with his own followers the supernatural occurrence of this event. It made an impression on him. He gave testimony to it. To have seen the heavens open like that had to have been breathtaking.

This event was a proclamation like no other made by God to His Son, "I love you. You please me." As the Spirit of God descended onto Jesus like a dove, God endorsed and verified to Jesus who He was in God's eyes. These words gave Jesus the emotional support He would need for the next phase of His life.

Jesus' first act before beginning public ministry was an act of obedience to Father God. He humbled Himself and was baptized by someone He created. Jesus came humbly and as a servant to show us the way to the Father, and the Father says, "That completely pleases me!"

The order of events here is very important. The Holy Spirit of God drove Jesus into the wastelands after He had received confirmation of who He was. This wilderness lay outside the boundaries of the flowing waters of the Jordan. It was dangerous, desolate, and deserted. The Spirit of God launched Jesus into a place of solitude, but the affirmation He had just received gave Jesus the courage to sail away from everything and walk into the desert. If I were about to go without food for 40 days I would also need some encouragement. Jesus knew who He was. God had just told Him. His identity was in place. He knew where He had come from. But the voice of His Father booming from heaven gave Him that extra boost of confidence He needed for the wilderness.

Wildernesses happen in each of our lives. They are places of loneliness. We find ourselves in neglected or abandoned regions. The wastelands that surround us are inhospitable. We need affirmation to survive these desert places. Sometimes we need to hear that we are valued as a person.

Do you ever watch the show "Running with Bear Grylls?" The renown survivalist invites celebrities to go away with him to various wildernesses across our globe. Their nutrition and lifegiving water comes from whatever nature may provide for them at the moment. I really don't think I could handle some of these situations they find themselves in.

Jesus was starring in His own version of the reality show, "Running with the Spirit." Jesus not only survived but He thrived in this desolation of brambles and ruins. He paved the way for us to follow in His path. It was a path He forged with the machete of the Word of God. He had been told "You are my Son and with You I am well pleased."

God has also spoken our identity into us. "But you are a chosen people, a royal priesthood, a holy nation, God's special possession, that you may declare the praises of him who called you out of darkness into his wonderful light" 1 Peter 2:9 NIV.

I am royalty! I am a child of the KING OF KINGS AND LORD OF LORDS! I am chosen by God. I am holy and set apart. I am God's special possession. He has a purpose for my life. I am supposed to declare the praises of God because He called me out of darkness. He called me out of the dark days of not knowing who I am or what I am supposed to do. God has told me to be the light on the hill. He has told me to be the salt of the earth. That is who I am and that is what I am supposed to do. We all need to find our true identity in Christ. When we know we are Children of God, we will survive our wilderness wanderings!

"You are the salt of the earth. But if the salt loses its saltiness, how can it be made salty again? It is no longer good for anything, except to be thrown out and trampled underfoot. You are the light of the world. A town built on a hill cannot be hidden. Neither do people light a lamp and put it under a bowl. Instead they put it on its stand, and it gives light to everyone in the house. In the same way, let your light shine before others, that they may see your good deeds and glorify your Father in heaven" Matthew 5:13-16 NIV.

The Floodgate of God's Joy

The Father watched from His throne in heaven as His Only Begotten was plunged into the waters of the Jordan. His heart swelled with uncontainable love for this Son of His. He heard the throne room echo with the prayer of His Child as Jesus' face broke the plane of the water. The Father God could no longer hold back the floodgate of emotion He felt as He observed this obedience from Jesus.

He reached down and rolled back the sky as one would a floor rug. A dove appeared in His hand as He brought it out from under His robe. The dove was a part of Himself. It was His Spirit. It was the very Spirit that hovered over the void on the day He created. God released that dove through the hole in the sky, and watched as it soared down to rest on the Love of His life.

His rich baritone voice rumbled out from the seat of His emotions. His voice was stirred from the deep well of His love. "You are my Son. You are My beloved. You delight me." This declaration resonated through the sky above, the earth beneath, and on into the caverns of the abyss.

Jesus heard that familiar voice of His Father. He cupped God's tangible presence into His hand as He cradled the dove near His bosom. The white bird was His promise. He could now face the dangers of this life. Those words infused Him with the courage and identity to thrive as He walked into the desolate brush with its thorns and thistles.

Waypoints to your destination:

What did God say to Jesus as He came up out of the water?

Why do you think that declaration was important?

Are you suffering from an identity crisis?

Who are you in God's eyes and what are you supposed to be doing?

"Lord, may each one of us remember who we are in Your eyes. Speak our identity into our hearts. Give us this encouragement so that we can thrive in the wilderness."

The Land of Temptation

Day Six

"Then Jesus was led by the Spirit into the wilderness to be tempted by the devil. After fasting forty days and forty nights, He was hungry. The tempter came to Him and said, "If you are the Son of God, tell these stones to become bread." Jesus answered, "It is written: 'Man shall not live on bread alone, but on every word that comes from the mouth of God.'"

Then the devil took Him to the holy city and had Him stand on the highest point of the temple. "If you are the Son of God," he said, "throw yourself down. For it is written: "'He will command His angels concerning You, and they will lift You up in their hands, so that You will not strike your foot against a stone.' " Jesus answered him, "It is also written: 'Do not put the Lord your God to the test.'"

Again, the devil took Him to a very high mountain and showed Him all the kingdoms of the world and their splendor. "All this I will give You," he said, "if You will bow down and worship me." Jesus said to him, "Away from Me, Satan! For it is written: 'Worship the Lord your God, and serve Him only.'" Then the devil left Him, and angels came and attended Him" Matthew 4:1-11 NIV.

Now the serpent was more crafty than any of the wild animals the Lord God had made. He said to the woman, "Did God really say, 'You must not eat from any tree in the garden?'"

The woman said to the serpent, "We may eat fruit from

35

the trees in the garden, but God did say, 'You must not eat fruit from the tree that is in the middle of the garden, and you must not touch it, or you will die.' "

"You will not certainly die," the serpent said to the woman. "For God knows that when you eat from it your eyes will be opened, and you will be like God, knowing good and evil." When the woman saw that the fruit of the tree was good for food and pleasing to the eye, and also desirable for gaining wisdom, she took some and ate it. She also gave some to her husband, who was with her, and he ate it," Genesis 3:1-6 NIV.

"So the Lord God banished him from the Garden of Eden to work the ground from which he had been taken. After He drove the man out, he placed on the east side of the Garden of Eden cherubim and a flaming sword flashing back and forth to guard the way to the tree of life" Genesis 3:23-24 NIV.

It is called the land of temptation. It's confusing to navigate through. There are many side roads offering myriads of delicacies to distract you as you travel along. It is difficult not to veer off and get side tracked. Each of us walk through this land every moment of every day. Adam and Eve were the first to travel through it. They lost their way and temptation swallowed them whole.

Jesus, however, was driven to this land by the Holy Spirit. He never stopped and He never swayed. Temptation kept throwing debris in His way. His path was littered with fool's gold and shiny rocks that glimmered like diamonds in the sun but were only cubic zirconium. Jesus kept His face toward the shining glory of His Father and conquered this land called temptation.

Eve and Jesus were tempted by the same enemy, Satan. He used the same modus operandi. He attacked the Word of God. Jesus was prepared because the Word of God was part of him.

Jesus was the Word of God made flesh. "In the beginning was the Word and the Word was with God and the Word was God. He was with God in the beginning" John 1:1-2 HCSB. Jesus triumphed over temptation when He said, "It is written..." The very word of God became His double edged sword over the attacks of the enemy.

Eve failed because she questioned the word of God. Eve succumbed when Satan asked, "Did God really say?" Her answer misquoted God's command to her. "And the woman said to the serpent, "We may eat fruit from the trees of the garden, except the fruit from the tree which is in the middle of the garden. God said, 'You shall not eat from it nor touch it, otherwise you will die'" Genesis 3:2-3 AMP. "And the Lord God commanded the man, "You are free to eat from any tree in the garden; but you must not eat from the tree of the knowledge of good and evil, for when you eat from it you will certainly die," Genesis 2:16-17 NIV. Eve attached an addendum onto the command, "nor touch it." Satan thrust though this open door. He was skilled in deceit and craftily made Eve doubt God's Word. She allowed the tempter a foothold into her thoughts. Eve didn't shield her mind with the Word of God.

When temptation came calling, Eve was thriving in the land of plenty and enjoying the animals Adam had named. When temptation came calling for Jesus, He was wandering in a desolate wasteland with wild animals on the prowl. Succulent fruit, ripe berries and running water were within an arm's length of Eve. Jesus roamed the dry barren desert with its brambles and thistles. It was a land without vegetation. Eve had everything tangible at her disposal, but failed to pull out her greatest weapon. Jesus who had nothing tangible at his disposal used his greatest arsenal, "The Word of God."

One was the Son of God; the other was created through the Son of God. Eve failed and was banished into the wasteland. An angel brandished a flaming sword to keep her from returning to the garden. Jesus triumphed and angels ministered continually to Him.

Jesus is our GPS system as we traverse through this land of temptation. Jesus said, "I am the way, the truth, and the life." Jesus showed us how to defeat the tempter. He gave us our greatest arsenal. He gave himself for He is the VERY WORD OF GOD.

The Tale of Two Temptations

The woman loved the garden. She wanted for nothing. She needed nothing for the garden supplied everything. The Creator made sure of that before He put her in the garden. The Creator took care of her. The fruit of every tree but one was within her reach.

The LORD GOD had taught them how to take care of it. The Garden of Eden was plush and vibrant green, and dotted with every color of food imaginable. Antioxidant rich food abounded throughout. Eve reached down to pluck a strawberry off the vine. She walked up to the orange tree and smelled the deep scent of citrus permeating the atmosphere. There were no dead bushes in this area. She ate her fill and when she became hungry again she just reached up and grabbed more fruit. When she thirsted, she cupped her hand and drank deeply from the flowing rivers that cascaded through the garden.

She had everything. She had the Presence of the Living God. He came and walked with them in the cool of the evening; all she had to do was call out to Him and He was by her side.

This garden was the place of her innocence until the serpent crept up. He was crafty. He took advantage of her. He came when she was vulnerable. She hadn't been on her walk with the Lord on this day. Her shield was down so he attacked.

"Did God really say...?" Eve didn't immediately rebuke him; instead she entertained his words. She allowed his words into her thoughts. She never pulled out The Word of God. She never quoted all the Creator had taught her on their walks. She didn't take command of the situation. Eve wasn't hungry, she had dined on a feast of fruits and vegetables just this morning; yet, she took a bite from the fruit that was offered to her.

Jesus was famished. The growl from his stomach was accentuated in the silence of the desert. He hadn't eaten in 40 days. A banana would sure taste good. He looked around. There was no color in this place. Deadwood littered the grayness of this wilderness. The terrain was uncultivated, uninhabited, and inhospitable. The landscape was against Him. This area was neglected and abandoned. It was a place of great danger. Jesus could feel the darkness lurking under the blowing tumbleweeds.

The very Holy Spirit of God had driven and guided Him to this place of temptation and chaos. Just as the children of Israel had followed the pillar of fire through the desert, Jesus had followed God's Spirit to these wastelands. He would make lemonade from lemons. Though He found Himself in this hostile terrain, He used it and drew strength from it. Instead of turning from the wilderness and crying bitterly, He relished in its solitude.

He turned to His Father moment by moment and minute by excruciating minute, allowing God to fill whatever He needed. "Father, Abba. You are in heaven and I am in this place now," He cried out to the gloomy sky above Him. As He prayed, Jesus felt the touch of His loving Father as if He was wrapped in an embrace.

39

His lips were parched and cracked. Jesus took a drink from the unseen well of God's living water. He feasted on bread from heaven when His stomach rumbled from starvation. Jesus infused and nourished Himself from the unseen platter of His Father's delicacies. He had become a man. He had the aches and pains and hunger of man, but He had seen it all before. He had heard man's bitter cries because they wanted more. When they had shouted for more, Jesus feasted on revelation from His Father.

In the wilderness, Jesus saturated himself with the Word of God. In the wilderness He got prepared for the tempter; for it wasn't if Satan would come, it was when Satan would attack.

Jesus sensed his vile presence before He saw it. Jesus knew his ways, and knew he slithered in the dark crevices of the dead bushes. Jesus had fought the attacks of the enemy since before creation. He was the One who had cast Lucifer out of heaven. Jesus had been there as the crafty one crept up to the woman.

Now, when He could smell his putrid form approaching Him in this inhospitable terrain, Jesus pulled out His weapon; it is the only weapon that would defeat the tempter; the very Word of God. "IT IS WRITTEN!" Jesus quoted words His Father had once written on stone. Jesus quoted His Father's Words which were given in a wilderness very much like this one. His steely words were born from desperate times, and He was desperately hungry. "It is written, man shall not live by bread alone."

When finally Jesus had enough, He commanded, "Away from me Satan for it is written, 'Worship the Lord your God and serve Him only.'" Jesus' voice came out loud and strong belying His weakened condition. The vile snake slithered away from Him for a season.

Waypoints to your destination:

According to Genesis 3, what were the mistakes Adam and Eve made in their temptation?

What was the final outcome of their failure?

What was the weapon Jesus used to defeat Satan?

What happened to Jesus after the snake slithered away?

Which outcome would you prefer?

"Lord, show me the way as I trudge through this land of temptation. Give me the desire to feast on Your Word. Prepare me so that I will be ready when I am tempted as You were."

The Battlefield

Day Seven

"A shoot will come up from the stump of Jesse; from His roots a Branch will bear fruit. The Spirit of the Lord will rest on Him – the Spirit of wisdom and of understanding, the Spirit of counsel and of might, the Spirit of the knowledge and fear of the Lord – and He will delight in the fear of the Lord" Isaiah 11:1-3 NIV.

"He will strike the earth with the rod of His mouth; with the breath of His lips He will slay the wicked. Righteousness will be His belt and faithfulness the sash around His waist" Isaiah 11:4-5 NIV.

"I saw heaven standing open and there before me was a white horse, whose rider is called Faithful and True. With justice He judges and wages war. His eyes are like blazing fire, and on His head are many crowns. He has a name written on Him that no one knows but He Himself. He is dressed in a robe dipped in blood, and His name is the Word of God. The armies of heaven were following Him, riding on white horses and dressed in fine linen, white and clean. Coming out of His mouth is a sharp sword with which to strike down the nations. "He will rule them with an iron scepter." He treads the winepress of the fury of the wrath of God Almighty. On His robe and on His thigh He has this name written: King of Kings and Lord of Lords" Revelation 19:11-16 NIV.

"And war broke out in heaven: Michael and his angels fought with the dragon; and the dragon and his angels fought, but they did not prevail, nor was a place found for them in heaven any longer. So the great dragon was cast out, that serpent of old, called the Devil and Satan, who deceives the whole world; he was cast to the earth, and his angels were cast out with him," Revelation 12:7-9 NKJV.

The battle had been ageless and bloody. Jesus had faced this enemy before and had defeated him soundly. Yet, here we go again. Matthew 4 in the NIV says, "Then Jesus was led by the Spirit into the wilderness to be tempted by the devil. After fasting forty days and forty nights, he was hungry. The tempter came to him and said, "If you are the Son of God..." Had he not been defeated enough? Was he a glutton for punishment? Did he think this would be any different? But yet, Satan tried one more time.

Each of Satan's attempts appeared to attack Jesus' true identity. "If you are the Son of God..." Satan accused. He came to Jesus at the point of Jesus' greatest weakness. The first attack appealed to immediate physical gratification. "You may eat right now by changing stones to bread." Then came the temptation for personal preservation. "You will not hurt Your foot." The last temptation appealed to lust for power and self-glory. "You will have all the world's kingdoms."

Our enemy is relentless. He has fought against Jesus since before creation, and at every turn he hounded Jesus as He walked this earth. Satan lurked in the dark shadows, and used the pride of the Pharisees and the greed of Judas Iscariot to attempt to throw Jesus off His true path.

Jesus was familiar with Satan's schemes though, and His weapons were sharpened and honed for the battle. He kept

His eye on the Father, and His ears open to the Father's words. The victory was His before the battle even began.

If Satan kept attacking Jesus, how on earth can we think he would be any less relentless in his attacks against us? The apostle Peter wrote:

"Be alert and of sober mind. Your enemy the devil prowls around like a roaring lion looking for someone to devour" 1 Peter 5:8 NIV.

We cannot think that Satan has slithered away and hid himself to no longer attack the creation of God. Peter warns us that Satan prowls around like a roaring lion. He is just waiting to pounce. Luke 4:13 in the NIV says, "When the devil had finished all this tempting, he left him until an opportune time."

He was just slinking in the dark shadows to attack Jesus again. We also, need to be prepared for the attack; arm ourselves as Jesus did, and realize Jesus has given us our victory chant, "It is written…"

The Place of Temptation

Jesus knew where the Spirit of God was driving Him, and knew the battle that lay ahead. The enemy was an age old opponent. Jesus had once called him, "Lucifer, the morning star." His Father had created this angel. Lucifer had once been an anointed cherub placed on the holy mountain of God. The memories came flooding back to Jesus as He looked onto the barren wasteland before Him.

Lucifer had been created by His Father in beauty to stand as guard to His Father, but a mean streak was found in Lucifer. It was blood red and filled with violence. This vein was sourced from Lucifer's pride because of his beauty. It flowed with the backed up stench of sewage and corrupted his wisdom with desire to overthrow The Father. His evil spread its spores to other created beings of heaven. The multitude of Lucifer's pride and lust profaned the sanctuary of heaven. He thought to exalt himself above the Father, but that is where his profanity ended. With eyes blazing, Jesus had thrown Satan out of heaven. His heart ached remembering the vision of His fiery darts consuming this enemy into chars of ash.

Now once again, Jesus smelled the smoldering aroma of burning excrement waffling His way. His body was weak for lack of food. Extreme hunger boiled in His stomach, but He girded up His core with the truth of God's Word and stood to face His ancient foe. The double edged sword was unsheathed from within Him. Satan may have sensed weakness but in truth these forty days of fasting had only strengthened His spirit. The nutrition that sustained Him these last forty days came from communion with His Father. The lack of food only made Him spiritually fit for the battle that was brewing on the horizon. He was the Field General. He had gathered His actionable intel, and His weapon was alive and active. The double edged blade of the Word of God was sharp, and Jesus knew how to wield it. He knew the precise points to penetrate His sword into this opponent.

Satan was masterful at deception and skillful with his manipulations. His pride in his cunning was his weapon of choice, but little did he know this pride would also be his downfall. He attacked at what seemed to be Jesus' weakness for the moment. "If you are the Son of God, tell these stones to become bread." Satan's vile breath oozed with greed. He thought to make Jesus question His identity. "Why would Your Father starve you?" Satan implied to Jesus. He pointed to the scattered rocks that looked like small loaves of bread. He kicked a stone to Jesus' feet. The temptation of immediate physical relief had worked once before on the woman, so he tried it again.

Jesus stepped over the stone putting it behind Him, and smiled to Himself. "I am the Son of God. I may not look like it on the outside, but I AM. My Father just spoke those words into me," He repeated the words to Himself to shield His thoughts from the onslaught of the deceit. The double edged sword sliced through His adversary's shoulder bringing a stain of blood right above the heart. "It is written..." Jesus spoke as the force of His Words penetrated the façade before Him.

Twice more Satan attacked Jesus' identity. He had heard the rumors of a masterful plan to save mankind. Now he was testing to see if these rumors were true. Would God allow His only Son to wrap Himself up into a man, become like them, just to save these creations? His hideous face belied his consternation over this plan. "If you are the Son of God..." he prefaced each temptation with that encompassing doubt. His resolve grew stronger after that first strike Jesus landed. He would not be defeated this time. Though his shoulder screamed of piercing pain, he pressed further.

It seemed as if the knife protruding from the mouth of Jesus grew sharper with each forceful Word. "It is written...," Jesus combated Satan's doubts, and with these words, the dagger sliced through the pride of Satan, that fierce dragon of old. Jesus' blazing eyes of fire bore a burning hole into the slanderous words that poured out of this decadent enemy. Satan's words flowed like a slime of filth, but Jesus' words were the song of victors. As He spoke the last, "It is written..." Satan slumped away defeated with blood dripping like a trail of tears.

"I will be back," Satan thought to himself. He slunk back into the abyss where he had come from. He would watch and *observe this man called Jesus, and he would wait for a more opportune time.*

Waypoints to your destination:

What does the bible call Satan in Matthew 4:3?

How did he attack Jesus?

What were Jesus' victory words?

How can you use this passage to stand firm in the face of your temptations?

"Lord, I put on my full armor of God so that I can stand in the face of the enemy's attacks. Fill me with Your Word."

Out of the Wilderness

Day Eight

"When the devil had finished every temptation, he temporarily left Jesus until a more opportune time. Then Jesus went back to Galilee in the power of the Spirit, and the news about Him spread through the entire region" Luke 4:13-14 AMP.

"So the devil left Jesus, and the angels came and took care of him" Matthew 4:11 NCV.

"Again, the next day, John was standing with two of his disciples. When he saw Jesus passing by, he said, "Look! The Lamb of God" John 1:35-36 NIV.

This was Jesus' entrance into public ministry. It was His cotillion and we have become invited guests. He marched out of the land of temptation a conquering hero, and He wore the victor's crown over all that would tempt us. Though he traveled through dry and barren terrain, He had a mountain top experience with the Lord God, His Father in heaven. When He spoke His last, "It is written," the devil scurried away from Jesus like the rat he truly was. When Satan exited, angels came and took his place. They soothed Jesus pains and hunger. They cooled Him with the flurry of their wings. He was the Commander of the Angel Armies and His soldiers were at His beck and call. Jesus couldn't stay in this comfortable setting. He had to leave the angels embrace because He didn't come to be coddled. Jesus came to serve, and He had to go to the lost sheep of Israel and become their sacrificial lamb. He was sent to become the Savior of the world. His feet would get dusty. He would get tired; yet, He resolutely placed one foot in front of the other and approached His starting blocks. Like Usain Bolt, He stretched his legs and squatted into his racing position.

He did a 360. He returned to the place of His baptism, the Jordan River. His energy was electric. He housed the Holy Spirit of God. The power of dynamite was bottled inside of Him. He was about to journey into the everyday lives of a hurting world. He went because He was sent. This was His first day on His new job, and He was intent on pleasing His Father.

This must also be our starting block for the race before us. We have also been sent to the lost and hurting people of the world. We are also filled with the Holy Spirit of God as we come into His presence, but those who come in must also go out. We need to travel to the mountain top and be filled with the Holy Spirit of God. We need to get our correct lane assignments. Then we also have to traverse down the mountain and run our race. After every vacation it is always hard to adjust to the real world, but God has set an amazing race for us to run. We need to go where He leads.

The Starting Blocks

He had been to the mountaintop. He had been filled. He hadn't eaten any nourishment, but He had been nourished by the Presence of the Living God, His Father, His Abba. He had won a great spiritual battle. He had defeated His eternal enemy by the very word of God. All He said was "Get out of here Satan," and the devil fled from Him. Angels came and took care of Him.

Jesus walked out of the wilderness completely saturated with the Holy Spirit of God. The power of God exuded throughout His entire body. His hands could heal, His mouth spoke wisdom, His spit restored sight, and His heart was filled with compassion that made Him ache for His creation.

His time had come. He must now enter the real world and show mankind who His Father really was. He knew the cost. He had weighed it before He had laid the foundation of the world. He had made His decision. His decision was made out of love and obedience to His Father in heaven. He could not leave fallen man in this wretched state.

He cinched up His sandals. He had become like them. He had come to restore them as He had created them; in His image. He had received His instructions for this day while He was in the wilderness. He must walk this way again. It had been forty days of gruel and hunger. It had been forty days of refreshment and filling. It was His paradox. He started where He had left off, back at the river where John had baptized Him, and the Spirit of God had come and filled Him. He started where He had heard His Father say, "You are my dearly loved Son and You bring me great joy." He lived to please His Father. His heart was full because He heard His Father express great delight in Him. This was His motive. This was the reason He got up in the mornings. This was His fuel.

Jesus saw John ahead of Him. He smiled. His cousin was still at it. Knee deep in the Jordan, John was immersing people into the river and calling them to repent. John was still doing what he had been called to do. John was the one to prepare the way for Jesus. John was His herald. He had run this race well, but the Field Judge had called for a new race to begin. John's course was about to change. He had ran in his correct lane, but now a new curve in the road was coming.

On the Way

"Look!" John shouted when he saw Jesus approaching. "The Lamb of God who takes away the sin of the world!" "He is the one I was talking about when I said, 'A man is coming after me who is far greater than I am, for He existed long before me.'" John knew he must decrease as Jesus must increase. This was his new set of instructions. Jesus heard John's proclamation there by the river and He was proud of His cousin. His heart was stirred because He saw the humility in this man who wore camel hair and ate locusts.

Kellye Jones

Waypoints to your destination:

After leaving the wilderness, how does the Bible describe Jesus in Luke 4:14?

Who attended to Jesus after the devil scurried away?

What were the words John used to describe Jesus as Jesus walked toward him?

John and Jesus ran different races, and ran them well. What is the race the Lord has called you to run?

"Father I come to you now. I want to get my right lane assignment. I want to run Your race. You are my Olympic coach. Lord, I come to this quiet place. Fill me with Your strength so that I might run as a marathon racer filled with Your endurance."

Exit Signs

Day Nine

"The following day John was again standing with two of his disciples. As Jesus walked by, John looked at him and declared, "Look! There is the Lamb of God!" When John's two disciples heard this, they followed Jesus. Jesus looked around and saw them following. 'What do you want?" He asked them. They replied, "Rabbi" (which means "Teacher") "where are you staying?" John 1:35-38 NLT.

"Andrew, Simon Peter's brother, was one of these men who heard what John said and then followed Jesus," John 1:40 NLT.

Do you know that split second moment when you have to make a decision to exit the freeway? Your GPS is giving you a vague, obscure direction, "Take the exit on your right." You look up and there are two exits off to the right – 4A and 4B. Which one? You're having that debate going off in your head, "This one or the next one?" You have to make a decision because you are about to cut someone off in the lane beside you. Your screaming at Grazelda, (the name I just gave my GPS voice because she annoys me just thinking about this scenario - no offense to anyone named Grazelda) "Which exit? Give me a number." That's the waypoint where we find Andrew in these verses in John 1. Andrew was a fisherman by occupation. He was the brother to Simon, whom we know as Peter, a disciple of Jesus. Andrew had come to this point at another time in his life. He had heard John the Baptist preach once, and he was convicted. He became a follower of John. And now, on this day standing on the shores of the Jordan, something in John's countenance made Andrew take another exit off this course. He started to follow Jesus.

"Look, the Lamb of God!" Notice the exclamation point. John's voice must have risen an octave. The sound rose a decibel and carried into the ears of Andrew. There had to have been conviction in John's words to cause two of his own faithful disciples to leave him. John was good with that. He knew he must decrease so that Jesus would increase. It was his own excitement and exclamation that sent Andrew seeking the Lamb of God. John refers his own disciples to Jesus. Ancient schools of teachers were sometimes competitive. Rarely were teachers so impressed with another teacher as to refer their students to them.

Four words spoken, "The Lamb of God." These words must have conjured up visions of temple sacrifices in Andrews thoughts as he walked away from John to follow this unknown Rabbi.

"And Aaron shall lay both his hands upon the head of the live goat and confess over him all the iniquities of the Israelites and all their transgressions, all their sins; and he shall put them upon the head of the goat [the sin-bearer], and send him away into the wilderness by the hand of a man who is timely (ready, fit)," Leviticus 16:21 AMP.

"The Lamb of God," hung as an exit sign above the path Andrew had been on. This exit sign loomed bright with promise and Andrew took it. From that day on he followed Jesus. He had no idea what that day held for him, but John's excitement propelled him to take the exit.

54

I have been called to point others to Jesus. So have you if you are a follower of Jesus. Am I speaking my testimony with such conviction and force that it causes others to follow after Him also?

That is what John did. He had seen the heavens open on the day he baptized Jesus. He had heard the testimony of God, "This is My Son!" John's eyewitness account of this event fortified his testimony.

I have my own eyewitness accounts of Jesus' magnificent works in my life, but do I speak them with the excitement and conviction of John's? Do my words speak life to other people? Do they cause people to exit their own paths to follow a path toward Jesus? Is my own testimony fortified by my personal account of Jesus working in my life?

Changing Directions

Andrew and Simon helped their father, Jonah, pull in the last of their fishing nets. The Sea of Galilee was like pure glass this early balmy morning. The three men coiled and hauled the fishing nets aboard their vessel. With backs aching from muscle strain they looked at the nights haul with weariness. A tempest squall had churned and swirled the Sea all night. They fought each wave with respect for that is what is required if you want to survive in this business. It had been a red moon at night and the sea did not want to give up its treasure of fish. The three fishermen were used to this. This had been their family business for all of their lives. From father to son, fishing had been handed down to each generation. Bethsaida was their home and fishing was their vocation.

Andrew and Simon walked along the shore after helping Jonah secure their fishing boat. John motioned for them to hurry. He and his brother, James, were also fisherman. They *were the sons of Zebedee and like Andrew and Simon, they helped their father fish. Fishing was their lives. Fishing was their profession, and each son loved it. They honored and respected their fathers and followed in their footsteps.*

Today was their day off. They were heading to the Jordan River where their teacher, John the Baptist, was baptizing. John was different than all other teachers in Israel. John taught that there was forgiveness and healing in repentance. Other teachers of their day, the Pharisees and scribes, liked to tack on extra strict rules as an addendum to the Laws of Moses making it impossible for the people of Israel to have any sort of relationship with the God of Abraham. They were too busy keeping the rules. John the Baptist taught a new way. "Repent, for the kingdom of heaven has come near," John cried out to those who came to him.

The four men found freedom in John's teachings. On their days off they followed after him. John sparked excitement in them because of his convictions of the coming of the Lord. The passion and fire in John invoked an expectancy in each of them. "Surely the long awaited Messiah will arrive soon," Andrew exclaimed as they walked the trails to the Jordan. The four detested the Romans traipsing through their beloved homeland. Every child of Israel looked to the horizon for their anointed king to come riding on a war horse and drive out the dreaded Roman empire. Their animosity for Rome was only exceeded by their contempt of the Jewish hierarchy and the religious demands that kept all Jews locked in a prison of laws.

Andrew, Simon, John and James desired true worship. That's why they followed John the Baptist. His words and their repentance brought freedom to their souls. They approached the Baptizer as he was taking a break.

On the Way

The Baptizer saw his disciples and came near to speak with Andrew and John. As he was talking to them, he got distracted. Andrew noticed John the Baptist's focus shift from their discussion and zero in on a stranger. Andrew could tell this man was a stranger to himself, but not to his teacher, John. Andrew noticed John's countenance visibly changed from passive to animated. Actually, could anyone describe John as passive? He always seemed animated and on high voltage but when John's gaze locked onto this man, Andrew visibly saw John's heart start speeding up.

Andrew felt as if he could see the words tumble out of John's mouth. "Look, the Lamb of God!" John exclaimed. Those were John's only words spoken to him and his friend, but they were the only words Andrew needed to follow this stranger. John spoke the words with such conviction, Andrew knew John had been an eyewitness to a spectacular sight. John's validation was all he needed to follow Jesus.

All the teachings of Moses flowed through Andrew's thoughts as he meditated on John's description of this man. "Who is this Rabbi he had started following? What compelled him to believe John's words?" Andrew thought to himself. He couldn't recognize the origin of this call, but he also couldn't ignore the desire to follow Him and see for himself.

Then the Rabbi turned, "What are you looking for?" "His eyes and His stare penetrate to my soul," Andrew thought to himself. It seemed the young Rabbi was asking for more than just a shallow answer, but it also seemed as if Jesus already knew the core reason Andrew was following Him. Andrew sensed at the end of this day he would receive more than he bargained for.

This was no ordinary Rabbi. Andrew saw it in His eyes. Andrew heard it in the Rabbi's question. These were ancient eyes filled with knowledge and wisdom. His was a voice that commanded life. "Rabbi, where are you staying?" Andrew heard himself ask.

Waypoints to your destination:

What do you think made Andrew start following Jesus?

What does John's description, "The Lamb of God," mean to you?

What does the exclamation point at the end of John's declaration mean?

Are you this passionate saying to others, "Look, The Lamb of God!"?

"Dear Lord, ignite a passion in me to point others to The Lamb of God. You have given me my own eyewitness account of Your greatness. Open doors that I can declare the works of God."

U-TURNS

Day Ten

"But Jesus turned, and as He saw them following Him, He said to them, What are you looking for? [And what is it you wish?] And they answered Him, Rabbi–which translated is Teacher–where are You staying?" John 1:38 AMP, classic edition.

"When possible make a legal U-turn." Yeah I hear that a lot from my GPS system. I turned right when I should have turned left, and I have to backtrack. Or, I don't notice a friend and I walk on by. She calls; I turn. We make these moves daily. We stop going one direction and turn to go the opposite direction. It's called a U-turn.

Jesus made several as He walked this earth. On this particular day He had already passed by John, Andrew, and his friend. He was going on in one certain direction, but then pivoted and went in the direction toward those who were following him. Andrew and his friend hadn't spoke to Him yet, but Jesus must have felt their presence behind Him. We aren't sure what caused Him to turn, but He did turn, and in that one U-turn, Jesus changed Andrew's life. The verses contained one subject matter, Jesus, and two verbs, turned and saw. These two sentences portrayed Jesus as a man of action. He was the initiator of this encounter. His first action; Jesus turned. He stopped his forward motion and pivoted, just so He could go toward Andrew and John, and not away from them. Jesus

59

hit the pause button and did not proceed on to the place where He was going. With this one pivotal action Jesus fulfilled a promise His Father made in Jeremiah 29:13 NLT, "If you look for me wholeheartedly, you will find me." God cannot deny His promises. Jesus changed directions so He could go toward two people who were seeking Him. Jesus' act of turning closed the gulf between them.

The second action Jesus took in these verses, "Jesus saw them following." Saw is a simple three letter word, but this verb sells the scene short. The Greek word for saw is, theaomai. It is the root word of our English word theatre. The definition is behold, contemplate, view attentively, to learn something by looking, to perceive, and lastly to visit.

The Psalmist says, "O LORD, you have examined my heart and know everything about me. You know when I sit down or stand up. You know my thoughts even when I'm far away" Psalm 139:1-2 NLT.

Andrew and his friend were on Jesus' examination table and He was the cardiologist sizing up the condition of their hearts. In that one look Jesus knew their true intent. He didn't need to perform an angiogram or take an X-ray. As one takes in a Broadway performance, Jesus viewed them intently as Andrew and his friend approached Him. The gap between them was closing. Jesus took in their body language, their countenance, and their stride. He surveyed the wholeness of their approach. They had left their former Rabbi, and followed in His footprints. They were true seekers.

It was His question that was the catalyst in this scene. Andrew and his friend were the first to follow after Jesus, but it was Jesus who spoke first in this encounter. "What are you looking for? What is it you wish?" His question made them do a self-examination. Were they looking for a revolutionary leader to overthrow Rome? Jesus was forcing them to define their purposes and goals.

Why were they following this man? All they knew at this point was their friend had called Him, "The Lamb of God," but something made them answer, "Rabbi – Teacher." Jesus had yet to teach them a single truth, and somehow they sensed He would.

A brief exchange had transpired between the three, but it was enough. They wanted to be taught by Jesus. The friends felt compelled to go the extra mile. Jesus had much in Him to offer them, and they wanted to hear His treasure of wisdom. They sensed an amazing adventure lay before them, so they sought to go where He traveled. Little did Andrew and his friend realize that day how their lives would be transformed by the Son of God.

Andrew's question was the equivalent of professing to Jesus, "Do not depart from us. Please, let us go where you are. Please, I want to be continually in Your Presence. I want to go where you are abiding." Andrew wanted to see Jesus' home. He wanted Jesus to be His teacher. It was a sincere and fervent request.

Andrew's question intimated a desire to become better acquainted with Jesus. Another biblical heroine once made this same request of her mother-in-law Naomi, "But Ruth replied, 'Don't urge me to leave you or to turn back from you. Where you go I will go, and where you stay I will stay. Your people will be my people and your God my God" Ruth 1:16 NIV.

It's called urgency, and Jesus honors it. He turns toward those who sincerely seek Him. It is time for me to inquire, "Rabbi, where are you staying?"

The U-Turn

Jesus could feel their stare. This day was about to pan out differently. A divine appointment was soon to interrupt this path, but He didn't mind the intrusion. The Son of God went with the flow of His Father. The voice of His Father spoke quietly into the recesses of Jesus' ear. "Turn toward them," God whispered to the Son. "They seek more than the legalism of their religion."

The Son of Man pivoted, made a u-turn and went toward those who sought Him. With the eyes of the Father, Jesus took them in. His gaze was intense. Their thoughts and desires could not be hidden from His knowing stare. "These are true sons of Israel," God spoke again.

They felt exposed, but still approached Him. "This man is peering into my deepest thoughts and wishes," Andrew thought to himself, but he didn't avert his gaze from the Rabbi's stare, nor did he change his pace. He walked steadily on toward the One he sought.

The air was charged with anticipation. The question broke the silence. "What do you desire?" Jesus asked them. God had already given Him the answer to this question, but He needed them to acknowledge and recognize their own true intent. They needed to hear it for themselves. They needed to own it. Andrew wanted to reach out and grasp hold of this Man who commanded his attention. "Where are you staying?" Andrew blurted out.

Waypoints to your destination:

What was the first action Jesus took when Andrew and his friend followed Him?

What does that action say to you?

How does Psalm 139 describe God?

What does Jeremiah 29:13 promise?

"Lord God, I come seeking you. I want more of you. God, You alone know my thoughts from afar. You know my true intentions. Give me Andrew's seeking heart."

The Place Where
He Was Staying

Day Eleven

"Come and see," He said. It was about four o'clock in the afternoon when they went with Him to the place where He was staying, and they remained with Him the rest of the day" John 1:39 NLT.

It was an invitation offered. "Come." It was the first of several invitations Jesus would offer this group. "Come follow me." "Come to me, all you who are weary and carry heavy burdens, and I will give you rest." Jesus tells Peter, "Come walk on water with me." John walking on the isle of Patmos on the Lord's day heard Jesus say, "Come up here, and I will show you what must take place after this" Revelation 4:1NLT.

Psalm 27:8 NLT, God says to the Psalmist, "Come and talk with me." In Isaiah 1:18 of the NLT God invites Israel, "Come now, let us settle the matter," says the Lord. "Though your sins are like scarlet, they shall be as white as snow; though they are red as crimson, they shall be like wool." "Come." It is a four letter word used to invite. The word invite comes from a Latin root word meaning "to go after something, pursue with vigor, or desire." The invitation was issued, but the RSVP was time sensitive. Come without delay and you will see. Right now is the time of acceptance. Jesus did not want them to miss this opportunity that would change their lives.

We issue invitations all the time. Kevin and I issued an invitation just the other night. "Can the boys (Asher and Lucas, our grandsons) come to the movies and spend the night with us?" Did you see the invitation, "Come?" We eagerly desired to go to the movies with our grandsons. We wanted to spend time with them. We wanted to share a movie experience and eat popcorn with them. "Zootopia" was calling, so we invited.

Jesus turned and saw two men honestly seeking to go with Him. So he implored them. "Come and you will see." At this point Jesus had performed no miracles; He owned no home; He didn't have a mortgage; He didn't pay insurance; He had no earthly permanent dwelling place. In fact Jesus once told His disciples, "Foxes have dens and birds have nests, but the Son of Man has no place to lay his head" Matthew 8:20 NIV.

He would offer these two no tea. He would cook them no meal, but ... He would give them words of abundance that abounded in grace. He would fill them with living water. He would feed them the Bread of Life.

All He saw in these two were seeking hearts. Jesus could see into their souls. Andrew and his friend wanted more from this life. They wanted truth. They craved real life, they wanted more than just the ritualistic religious practices of the Pharisees. Jesus gave them all they wanted and more.

They stayed with Jesus for the rest of the day. Oh to have been a fly on that wall. Wouldn't you have loved to be privy to that conversation? Where did Jesus take them? Where was He staying at this time? What furniture did they sit on? I don't know. The bible doesn't say, but I do know the meeting was vivacious. It was rapturous. The teaching had to enthrall them. I know this because they remained with Jesus for the rest of the day. The words Jesus offered held their attention. They weren't looking at their watches with distraction. They weren't getting texts or emails that made them avert their eye gaze. No. They were wrapped up in infatuation with the Teacher. Jesus had issued an invitation, they accepted, and He had an attentive audience.

Another invitation was always looming before Jesus since before the foundations of the world were laid. The cross beckoned, "Come, Jesus. Pay the price." He accepted. The empty tomb that was chiseled into the mountain that He created sang out to Him, "Come, here is Your Victory." The tomb was His abode for three days and three days only. On the third day He vacated that lodging place. Up from the grave He arose.

How many times in my life have I had that invitation offered to me? When my two girls were little they would invite me, "Come have a tea party with us!"

After Kevin lost his father, our son invited Kevin, "Come to Pittsburgh and celebrate Father's Day with us." In both instances we accepted. We were enthralled and gave each our rapt attention.

Jesus issues the same invitation to us daily. Just a moment ago I walked down the hall and read our family creed that Kevin had engraved into a plaque, "Let us come boldly to the throne of grace that we may obtain mercy and find grace in our time of need" Hebrews 4:16 NIV. That was Jesus' invitation to me this morning. Time for me to turn off my iPhone, silence the texts and the emails, turn off Facebook, and shut out all other distractions.

My Savior wants me to sit with Him awhile. He wants to share things with me. He wants to teach me great and unsearchable things I cannot learn on my own. He and He alone has the words of life that I need for my day. His conversation is vivid with promises of help. His words tell these dry bones to rise up. They fill the vacant places of my soul, and become my vitamins of vitality.

The Lodge

It wasn't much. No king or Caesar would ever lay their head in this place. The furniture was sparse, and the inn was modest. Andrew could tell this lodging wasn't a permanent dwelling. This upper room held no baggage or personal possessions. Jesus wasn't the type to plant roots, or be ladened with material goods which would slow him down. No, there was something different about the One that Andrew had just called Rabbi. Jesus was the itinerate preacher going from town to town as He felt led. Jesus was a stranger and a foreigner who walked this planet earth. His true home came from another origin, but Andrew didn't care. Jesus had an aura of a learned sage that permeated His whole demeanor. Andrew followed Jesus because no other Rabbi had ever impressed Andrew like this Rabbi. When Jesus invited him, Andrew accepted.

After climbing the outside steps, Jesus opened the door and led them into the room. With arms open wide He invited them to come in. "Sit down, rest here," Jesus implored. Andrew entered first and sat on the floor by the Master's feet. He had been exhilarated from the earlier conversation as they walked along, and now, he was planted in rapt attention and prepared to listen to every word from Jesus' mouth. The room may have been mundane, but the teaching was exhilarating. In Jesus' presence the things of this earth seemed to fade away.

Andrew was drawn to Jesus' excellence. Jesus' words and personality were charismatic and filling. His teachings were like diamonds across black velvet. Jesus didn't offer them worldly advantage; Jesus offered them life abundant. Andrew was meant to be here in the presence of this new Rabbi.

Waypoints to your destination:

What was the invitation Jesus offered?

Why do you think Jesus invited Andrew and his friend to His place of lodging?

What did Andrew do once the invitation was given?

How long did these two stay with Jesus?

Lord, "Just as I am, without one plea, but that thy blood was shed for me, and that thou bids me come to thee, O Lamb of God, I come, I come."

Four O'Clock

Day Twelve

"Come and see," He said. It was about four o'clock in the afternoon when they went with Him to the place where He was staying, and they remained with Him the rest of the day. Andrew, Simon Peter's brother, was one of these men who heard what John said and then followed Jesus. Andrew went to find his brother, Simon, and told him, "We have found the Messiah" (which means Christ) John 1:39-41 NLT.

Do you ever wonder if the Bible is credible? Is it just a book filled with fantasy stories based upon the life of a man named Jesus? Scholars have argued this dilemma throughout the centuries. Some claim the gospels were written hundreds of years after the fact. Historians search for eyewitness credibility.

Philosophers through the ages have questioned the gospel's validity because they do not believe these documents were composed by Jesus' disciples or any first century Christian. I see many hiccups in these theories. The greatest flaw that I see in these was Jesus' influence. What Jesus did and what Jesus said sparked a chain reaction in the culture of mankind that has lasted over two thousand years. He ignited a social movement that spread across the Roman Empire. His influence was massive and it couldn't have been mythical. The Under-ground movement He started changed the course of human history. His laws and standards even inspired our

Declaration of Independence. The second paragraph of the United States Declaration starts as follows, "We hold these truths to be self-evident, that all men are created equal, that they are endowed by their Creator with certain unalienable rights, that among these are Life, Liberty and the Pursuit of Happiness."

So, call Jesus of Nazareth the most interesting man in the world, but don't call Him mythical.

I actually do not question the authenticity of the Bible. I do see an eyewitness accountability embedded in John 1:39. "It was about four o'clock in the afternoon" John 1:39 NLT. The Teachers Bible Commentary denotes that John, the writer of the gospel of John, was the other friend of Andrew's. Two friends who had once been disciples and students of John the Baptist, left to follow after this new teacher. "It was about four o'clock in the afternoon," John writes in this gospel. John put a time stamp at the exact moment he decided to follow Jesus. Only an eyewitness to this event would be able to do that, and know exactly what time he experienced Jesus.

It had been a whole evening spent with the Son of God. From four in the afternoon until the next morning, Andrew and John had sat at the feet of this great Teacher. Jesus was the one who created the world, so He knew the law of physics. Jesus was there when the first breath had been blown into the first man, Adam; He knew how to heal mankind's ailments. Andrew and John now found themselves listening to the teachings of the Ancient of Days. Four o'clock in the afternoon that day made an impression on John. He recorded it for us. At four o'clock in the afternoon, John's life changed forever. He walked out of that lodge knowing he was loved, in fact six times throughout the gospel he called himself the beloved disciple.

Jesus had invited them, "Come and you will see." He made Himself available to mankind. Jesus obviously liked spending an entire evening with Andrew and John. Jesus talked with them and associated with them. Maybe they sat around a fire and shared a meal in this guest room. This was the beginning place of the relationship He was about to build with these two. Coincidentally, one of the last places Jesus would bond with them was also an upper guest room of another house. Jesus left His home in heaven for such times as these.

Whatever you want to call it, don't call it a casual meeting, and don't call it rushed. They remained with Jesus the rest of the day. Casual and rushed defines some of my quiet moments with Jesus. I meet with Him a cursory 15 minutes before I begin rushing around for the day. It's not much time to influence the trajectory of my day.

Jesus' last four words of invitation were, "and you will see." A person must come to Jesus before they will see Him. These two came, then got more than they bargained for. When Andrew and John began that day, they had no idea it would end sitting at the feet of the One who created them. The invitation didn't include full belief in Jesus. All Jesus promised here was they would see and experience a new adventure. This was a beginning step for these two. A fire was about to be lit in their souls. It started with just embers but it would eventually become a flame that would be passed along.

I don't know what was said or what Jesus shared and revealed during those hours, but I do know the outcome. Andrew was inspired by what he saw and heard. The words exchanged convinced him that he had been in the presence of the Messiah, his Messiah, so he responded. He told his brother Simon Peter, "We have found the Messiah," John 1:41 NLT. John and his brother James also became followers of Jesus.

Jesus called these two "sons of thunder." "James and John (the sons of Zebedee, but Jesus nicknamed them "Sons of Thunder,) Mark 3:17 NLT.

Andrew and John's life changed dramatically at four o'clock that day. When they set out on this journey from Bethsaida to the Jordan River to listen to their teacher, John the Baptist, they had no idea how their lives would be transformed because they met with the Son of God.

I do not think it was the quantity of time spent with Jesus as much as it was the quality of time spent with Jesus. It was the fact that Jesus allowed for this interruption into His day. He did a U-turn and approached Andrew and John. He initiated the conversation and He offered the invitation.

Jesus left His permanent home in heaven and He came and took up temporary residence among the people of this world just to bridge the gap between His Father and His creation. He invited them and He invites us still, "Come in and You will see."

Eight O' Clock

I stared at the ceiling with a heavy heart. It had been a long Sunday. As always, my parents took me and my baby brother to church. We attended Sunday School together, big church, and then Sunday night church. At age eight those were my descriptions of Sundays.

This Sunday night after all festivities of the day were concluded, it felt different. I felt different. I was burdened. Things were not right in my heart and in my soul. Again, I was eight years old, I really didn't listen to the preacher in big service, but the song kept playing in my head. "Fill my cup Lord. I lift it up, Lord. Come and quench this thirsting in my soul..." A tear slid down my cheek as I sang this song again at eight o'clock in the evening of that Sunday when my life was changed.

My mom came to check on me when she heard my quiet sobs. I tried to put words to my deep feelings. How does an eight year old explain to their mom that they recognized their need of a Savior? I guess you call it a mother's intuition, but she got it. My dad came in and we prayed together. The next day I went to visit with the preacher man whose sermons I never really listened to and he explained to me the gospel message of God's saving grace. He used terms an eight year old could understand. He had me pray and confess my great need. I needed forgiveness and what I got was an eternal home.

That was almost fifty years ago, but I remember it like it was yesterday. I have it time stamped in my memory. One Sunday night at eight o'clock, I became a follower of Jesus.

Waypoints to your destination:

What time was it when Jesus invited Andrew and John to, "Come and see?"

What did Andrew and John do when they received the invitation?

Did this meeting change their lives and what makes you think so?

Have you had that time stamp on the moment Jesus changed your life? If not what's holding you back?

"Lord, thank You for inviting me to come and see. I have seen and tasted that the Lord is good."

Seeking His Brother

Day Thirteen

"Therefore go and make disciples of all nations, baptizing them in the name of the Father and of the Son and of the Holy Spirit, and teaching them to obey everything I have commanded you. And surely I am with you always, to the very end of the age" Matthew 28:19-20 NIV.

We know this verse as The Great Commission. The resurrected Jesus spoke these last words to His disciples on a mountain in Judea just before His ascension into heaven. He tells them, "Go." It is a simple action verb comprised of two letters, but embedded in the command is another implied command. Before a person can go anywhere, that said person must have come from somewhere. The key to obeying The Great Commission is coming into the Presence of God first. In God's Presence we soak up all that He is. His Spirit fills us with a passion to go.

"The first thing Andrew did was to find his brother Simon and tell him, 'We have found the Messiah.'" ("Messiah" means "Christ.") Then Andrew took Simon to Jesus" John 1:41-42a NCV.

The precept above was fulfilled when we see Andrew seek out his brother Simon. The fellowship and camaraderie Andrew experienced during his encounter with Jesus charged him to go; go and search out his brother. Andrew was on a mission and he would not be distracted. So, Andrew became the first missionary. He sped off to find Simon. The journey Andrew began the day before culminated with a passion to introduce his brother to Jesus. His expectations had been out-done the moment Jesus began teaching. There was no other option for Andrew but to go.

Five words of declaration, "We have found the Messiah," were the only words spoken by Andrew, but they were the only ones needed. He preached a sermon to his brother not with words but with actions, and by bringing Simon to Jesus, he did the church a great service. Words were needless to Andrew, actions were his agenda.

The gospel of John speaks of Andrew twice more in John 6:4-9 and John 12:20-22. Both times he was bringing someone to Jesus. This was the result of the effect Jesus had on him. He spent a whole day in conversation with Jesus, and Andrew had been filled. He had tasted that the Lord is good, so he felt obliged to go and tell.

The fellowship that occurred in that room between Andrew, John, and Jesus was not an encounter to be monopolized. They had an authentic tangible interaction, and it convinced Andrew of a deeper conviction. John the Baptist only characterized Jesus as the "Lamb of God." Andrew declares one step further, "We have found the Messiah."

Palestine at this time was experiencing a religious revival. The Pharisees were calling for strict adherence to the Law of Moses and tacking on unachievable addendum's to these Laws. John the Baptist strode through the countryside calling all to repentance and a true relationship with Yahweh. Israel was expecting their long awaited Messiah, their deliverer, the Anointed of God. The prophet Isaiah had written about Him centuries earlier. The day Andrew had spent in the presence of Jesus convinced him that he had found Israel's Messiah. This was his conclusion that he declared to Simon. It was one step deeper than his former teacher had taken.

Andrew was a dependable behind the scenes kind of guy. Simon would become Peter the evangelist of the first century church, but it was Andrew's humble attitude that started Simon on his journey. "We have found the Messiah," Andrew proclaimed to Simon. He would not take the credit for this discovery all for himself. Andrew rejoiced in the fact he and a friend had followed Jesus.

This is the outcome of quality time spent with our Deliverer. We go and we tell. We preach by our actions; we speak with humility and praise about the One who saved us.

"When we tell you these things, we do not use words that come from human wisdom. Instead, we speak words given to us by the Spirit, using the Spirit's words to explain spiritual truths" 1 Corinthians 2:13 NLT.

"For when we brought you the Good News, it was not only with words but also with power, for the Holy Spirit gave you full assurance that what we said was true. And you know of our concern for you from the way we lived when we were with you" 1 Thessalonians 1:5 NLT.

The First Missionary

Andrew and John had been satiated. A whole day had been spent listening to this Rabbi. Jesus's words fell like balm onto their parched souls. For so long Andrew and John had been pummeled with religious laws that kept them longing for a true relationship with Yahweh, but Jesus' words penetrated and filled the vacuum that the law left in its wake. Andrew's thoughts were swirling with a singular mission. He must find his brother Simon.

Andrew and John had left their brothers at the shores of the Jordan. They alone followed after the man from Nazareth, Jesus of Galilee. Simon and James had stayed behind enthralled with the Baptist scathing accusations against the Pharisees and Sadducees. "You brood of vipers," John the Baptist's declarations rang out. Simon and James were hooked; they stayed behind to see how this would play out.

Andrew and John had chosen the greater path. They followed the Galilean to a guest house and had been filled to overflowing from His discussions of unseen things from above.

Andrew was convinced. This was his Messiah, the Anointed of God. It was crucial now. He must bring his brother to Jesus. These past two days did not end in the manner he expected. When he left his father, Jonah, at the dock yesterday, he had no idea who would be waiting on him at the end of this path. He was one of the first to recognize the long awaited promise of God. He had been in the presence of Jesus the Christ, the consolation of Israel. The words of Jesus had fallen like winds of peace onto Andrew's ears. With haste and purpose, he walked off to find Simon.

Waypoints to your destination:

What was the first thing Andrew did after being in the presence of Jesus?

How did Andrew describe Jesus to Simon?

What did Andrew do after finding Simon?

What do you think is the key to the Great Commission?

"Lord, give me the courage and the boldness to bring others to You. Lord fill me with Your Presence"

Follow Me

Day Fourteen

"Then Andrew brought Simon to meet Jesus. Looking intently at Simon, Jesus said, "Your name is Simon, son of John – but you will be called Cephas" (which means "Peter") John 1:42 NLT.

Andrew had found that pearl of great price. All of Israel had been seeking their anointed king who would rule again over the House of David, and Andrew and John had found Him. They had an encounter with the living God and it propelled them to go and tell.

Simon was the first person Andrew thought of to go and tell. He knew right where Simon was, so he made a bee line for him. Simon was family and family was his first obligation. I quote Lilo from the movie "Lilo and Stitch," "Ohana means family. Family means nobody gets left behind or forgotten." Simon was very dear to Andrew and he would not leave him behind.

He brought his brother to the fountain of wisdom. Andrew did not presume to speak much. He let Jesus' words be the converter. The day he had spent with Jesus and the conversation that followed affected Andrew and propelled his tone and voice. All he spoke to Simon, "We have found the Messiah!" His conversation was littered with power because he had been with Jesus. Andrew's words must have stirred Simon's curiosity for he followed his brother. They were five words spoken as an imperative. They were like opposite ends of a magnet. Andrew led, Simon followed. These five words spoken with conviction persuaded Simon to seek the truth of his brother's encounter.

Simon went looking for God's anointed and he too, was not disappointed. No introduction takes place. None was needed. Jesus looks at this total stranger and says, "You are Simon, son of John." Andrew never pointed out this was his brother. Jesus just offered proof to these new acquaintances that He was omniscient, and He still is all-knowing, all-seeing, and all-wise. Upon first sight, Jesus knew Simon's name and his father's name.

When we first meet people, what is the first thing we ask of each other? Most often it is, "What is your name?" We then make further inquiries. We get to know each other. Our omniscient Savior needs no introduction. He knows our name. Jesus knows our character and He knows our every thought according to Psalm 139.

Then, there are those first few seconds of engagement between Simon and Jesus. Can you not picture this scene in your mind? It was the game of "Who blinks first?" Jesus looked up to give Simon a considerate acknowledgement. His gaze was locked in on Simon. His look was concentrated and fixed on Simon's potential. Jesus knew Simon's character, and He knew Simon's destiny.

Jesus' look held great love and concern for this ordinary fisherman. Jesus took time to consider more than what was physically visible. Others may have seen a struggling fisherman from the shores of Galilee, but Jesus saw in Simon a rock upon which His church would one day be built. Jesus saw past the failures and mistakes this man would make. He saw and beheld a man who contained a sure foundation.

Jesus stared at Simon intently, and broke the ice, "You will be called Cephas." Cephas is Aramaic for rock. Jesus spoke into being that which was not seen by ordinary eyes. This shifting sand of a man would one day be a firm foundation for His church.

This meeting with Jesus was a life transforming event for Simon. Jesus renamed him. He was Simon which meant obedient. He was Simon bar Jonah, Simon son of John. Jesus made Simon his own when he renamed him. Jesus adopted Simon into His forever family.

Peter was an impetuous, stiff necked, and out spoken disciple of Jesus, but Jesus transformed him. His life morphed into the rock of the first century church. Jesus transformed Simon into Peter, a person of a strong and firm faith that would lead others long after He Himself had left this world.

That is what Jesus does in the life of those who believe in Him. He changes us. He calls us new creations. He sees in us what the world cannot see. Jesus saw beyond Simon's horizon, and in calling Peter, Jesus saw a rock who would build a dynasty of followers.

God never views us as we view ourselves, nor for that matter, as our society views us. God sees greatness in us. God sees what we could become if we would just give our lives over to Him.

The Rock

Simon had been discouraged as he approached the lodge where Jesus had chosen to stay. There was no opulence to this place. It was pure simplicity. Kings and emperors would bypass these doors, yet, in this house the Messiah, Israel's anointed, resided. That was what Andrew claimed any way.

Then came the moment. Andrew opened the door. Jesus the Messiah stood to honor the new guest. The atmosphere was electric with anticipation; Andrew even sucked in his breath. His brother stood frozen waiting for the exchange to take place. The whole encounter was mesmerizing. Simon couldn't turn away from those eyes that seemed to penetrate his soul. There were no words to describe the anxiety he felt as Jesus spoke his name.

There was some mysterious wonder that stirred his heart as he heard his name called out by this Man before him. A spark was lit and a flame began to burn in his gut. Somehow in this first greeting, he knew an adventure lay before him that was much greater than anything he could ever dream.

Jesus heard His Father's whisper, and remembered the charge He had received before leaving heaven. He knew the twelve whom He would choose even before this day occurred. He had been given His Father's eyes to see past the façade of physical appearance. The moment Simon entered the room Jesus saw the rock He would build His church upon. He knew this man who just entered His dwelling, knew who his father was, and more importantly, He knew who Simon would become. "You are Simon, son of John. You will be called Cephas!"

Waypoints to your destination:

Why do you think it was so important for Andrew to lead his brother to Jesus?

Why do you think Simon followed his brother?

What happened the moment Simon met Jesus?

How does this encounter affect your everyday life?

"Lord, I come to seek you. Lord where are you staying? Jesus come abide in me. I want to follow after You."

Heading North

"The next day Jesus decided to go to Galilee," John 1:43 NCV.

The journey begins with six men. Andrew and his brother Simon, John and his brother James, began following Jesus at the Jordan River. The next day Jesus determines to go to Galilee. He seeks out Philip who then brings Nathanael. A fantastic voyage awaits them. They just don't realize how amazing it will become. From the moment they take the first steps to follow, a swirling frenzy of epic proportion unfolds before them. Each and every new event brought jaw dropping miracles that were difficult to understand and even harder to explain.

Turn the page, as we travel with them, "On the Way"

It will be a timeless journey that has survived thousands of years.

Jaw dropping experiences lie ahead.

Leave your bags at the door. You can't prepare for the adventure ahead. Just take that first step to follow, be present, be attentive, and most of all be available.

The House of Nets

Day Fifteen

"On the next day Jesus wanted to set out for Galilee. He found Philip and said to him, "Follow me." (Now Philip was from Bethsaida, the town of Andrew and Peter.) John 1:43 NET.

The circle was expanding. The net spread wider as Jesus threw it out there. More men were beginning to buy into the His teachings. Jesus' philosophies were radical. They were not the same brand of strict adherence to the Law of Moses as the other Rabbi's were teaching. The words that poured forth from this Rabbi were sprinkled with grace and not religion.

Jesus had just come from His wilderness experience. He walked by the shores of the Jordan River. Four men followed after him. First Andrew and John the author, then Andrew brought his brother, Simon Peter, and possibly John brought his brother, James.

The next day dawned bright and sunny, and Jesus decided to head to Galilee. Jesus was never whimsical. Every footstep He took was intentional. When Jesus set out for Galilee on this day, He knew it was His Father's will for Him at this time. He was to follow the Jordan River north to the Sea of Galilee. "My food," said Jesus, is to do the will of Him who sent me and to finish His work" John 4:34 NIV. Jesus desired to go to Galilee. On now this third day after His baptism, Jesus intentionally sat out to find Philip. He didn't waste any time in this gathering process. Jesus' days on earth were short. He had to cast His net and begin gathering His followers. His Father's work was His business. Pleasing His Father was His sole desire, and He would not loose a day.

The count was slowly growing. What began with two was now increasing person by person. It wasn't the quantity that mattered, it was the quality Jesus sought.

Philip was next on the gathering list. It wasn't a game of hide and seek. Jesus didn't go searching. He knew who He would call before He ever left heaven. He knew the ones His Father had given Him, so He sat out on a journey to call them. The word "find" implies that the meeting was not accidental. It was the same word that was used in Luke 19:10 of the NIV, "For the Son of Man came to seek and to save the lost." Jesus was gathering the lost sheep of Israel who had been led astray by the hierarchy of Jewish religion.

On the third day of this Amazing Race, five men were now following. Three of them had something in common. Andrew, Simon Peter, and now Philip were from the town of Bethsaida. Bethsaida was a fishing town on the shores of the Sea of Galilee. It's name signified "House of Nets." Jesus was calling fishermen. He wasn't calling the professors and the students of higher leaning in Mosaic Law. He was calling the blue collar workers of Jewish society. Bethsaida was on the northeast side of the Sea of Galilee, and had a reputation for being a wicked place.

"Woe to you, Shoran! Woe to you, Bethsaida! For if the miracles that were performed in you had been performed in Tyre and Sidon, they would have repented long ago in sackcloth and ashes" Matthew 11:21 NIV.

God has always had a remnant of followers no matter the deprivation of the current society. Even in Bethsaida, Jesus found soil to plant His teachings. The blue collar workers in Jewish population had the reputation of being shallow and just following the status quo of their religion, but Jesus saw in these fishermen learners who would be responsive, and He offered these His best.

"Follow me," Jesus tells Philip. For some reason Philip does. An offer based off two words, and Philip accepts. He follows Jesus out his door and onto the road before him.

Jesus' words had the power to compel people to move. On the day of His arrest, Jesus spoke the words, "I Am" and a legion of Roman soldiers fell faint at His feet. "Follow me," and Philip was prepared to follow. Just think of all that Philip would have missed out on had he not chosen to follow Jesus on this particular day.

Jesus was participating in an amazing race. It was a journey His Father had prepared for Him. He had waypoints on the way to His final destination. Golgotha's hill lay at the end of this road, but the glory afterwards was well worth the cost.

On the way Jesus cast out a net to gather His followers. He spoke words of grace and truth that ignited a passion for more of Him. One by one they followed this Pied Piper onward in this amazing race. I can't even begin to explain their loss had they not followed. They would never have lived the grand adventure of seeing water turned to wine or witnessing the blind see again or watching the dead rise up.

These men who were following Jesus had their flaws for sure. They would make many mistakes. They would even doubt His power, but they had one thing going for them. They followed when He offered the invitation.

The initiation always began with Jesus. Jesus was sent to bridge the gulf between man and his Creator. Jesus had that charismatic personality. He loved those He created and He enjoyed being around them. He was a people person, and He would draw all men to Himself.

This small band of brothers would grow to twelve, who would then grow to thousands, but He kept this group small and intimate. He would share Himself with them. They were on a road trip and Jesus was the guide. Oh, the things that they would see, and the words they would hear. Their lives were enriched because they followed Jesus of Nazareth.

Jesus is the same yesterday, today and tomorrow. His calling is still as powerful. His love still as deep. Oh the adventure you will miss if you don't heed His words, "Come, follow me."

The Day Jesus Came Calling

"Lord, show us the Father." As soon as he asked the question, the accusations came flying into his thoughts. Why did he always have to be the one to question? Why did he always have to have tangible, physical evidence of Jesus' identity?

Philip remembered the day he helped gather twelve baskets of leftovers after Jesus' had fed five thousand people with five small barley loaves and two small fish. He had put voice to his doubts on that day also. His dogmatic statement to Jesus floated to his memory, "It would take more than a half a year's wages to buy enough bread for each one to have a bite!"

Philip knew his true nature. He was skeptical and materialistic, but Jesus of Nazareth, Son of God, and Son of Man was able to create greatness out of little.

His parents had been influenced by the Greek culture of his hometown. They had given him a Grecian name and not a true

Hebrew name, yet, for some unknown reason the Carpenter from Nazareth came to his house, and he had been pulled like an iron to a magnet that day Jesus had knocked on his door. "Follow me," Jesus had requested, and Philip did. Being a hardworking fisherman, he had been honored this traveling Rabbi had come seeking him out. How could he not follow the Lamb of God, as John the Baptist had described Him?

That day had seemed like yesterday even though months had passed. Everyday had been filled with excitement, curiosity, wonder, and magnificence. He wouldn't have missed this journey for the world, but still he couldn't help himself. He had to ask the tough questions.

"Don't you know me by now, Philip, even after I have been among you such a long time?" Jesus' question brought Philip back to the here and now.

Waypoints on the way:

How was Philip's calling different from Andrew's and Peter's?

How do you think Philip felt that day Jesus said, "Follow me?"

Do you ever feel too inadequate to be a follower of Jesus?

How have you questioned Jesus' power to transform you?

"Lord, You have invited me to follow You. Lord transform me. Help me to represent You to the world."

Under the Fig Tree

Day Sixteen

"Philip went to look for Nathanael and told him, "We have found the very person Moses and the prophets wrote about! His name is Jesus, the son of Joseph from Nazareth." "Nazareth!" exclaimed Nathanael. "Can anything good come from Nazareth?" "Come and see for yourself," Philip replied.

As they approached, Jesus said, "Now here is a genuine son of Israel – a man of complete integrity." "How do you know about me?" Nathanael asked. Jesus replied, "I could see you under the fig tree before Philip found you."

Then Nathanael exclaimed, "Rabbi, you are the Son of God – the King of Israel." Jesus asked him, "Do you believe this just because I told you I had seen you under the fig tree? You will see greater things than this." Then he said, "I tell you the truth, you will all see heaven open and the angels of God going up and down on the Son of Man, the one who is the stairway between heaven and earth" John 1:45-51 NLT.

I love bumping into friends when I'm out. It makes you feel part of a community where everybody knows your name. It's kind of hard in bigger cities to run into people that you know. You have to break down your city into smaller groups like at church, gym, work, school pick-up lines, or common interest groups. I came home from the gym the other day feeling pretty good about myself. I knew at least six people and they knew me. In fact they called out my name. We, as a created people, need that sense of community. We need to feel we belong.

Jesus knows this, and that is what we find Him doing as He traveled through the Judean countryside. He was creating community from a small sector of men. These men whom Jesus gathered on this walk became part of a group that had first hand communion with the Lord. Each person who came into the fold discovered a deeper truth about Jesus that would take them further and further into the rabbit hole that led them to their wonderland.

They had widely different temperaments and personalities. James and John were known as Sons of Thunder. Simon Peter and Andrew, though brothers, were as different as any two you would meet. One boisterous in his devotion to Jesus, the other working quietly behind the scenes to be a servant to his Lord. Now Philip joined up with the group. Jesus had specifically sought him out.

Jesus would knit them together in unity. He called them each by name, and helped them to believe in who He was. Their belief became their cord of belonging. Only Jesus knew where they were heading and what was in store for them, but they followed when He invited them to come. Each person responded in various ways, and Philip responded by finding his friend Nathanael.

"We have found the very person Moses and the prophets wrote about!" Philip explains to Nathanael in John 1:45. Philip had just spent enough time with Jesus to discover this fact. It wasn't his discovery alone. Philip gave credence to his exclamation by adding in witnesses. "We have found..." He was excited to share it. His fact finding mission ended with this declaration, "His name is Jesus, the Son of Joseph from Nazareth." Each person's description of Jesus was as different as their personalities. All were true statements, just different perceptions of the same man.

Now we add one more to the mix. Nathanael, the one that Jesus described as a true Son of Israel, had selective hearing at this point. All he heard was, "Jesus, the son of Joseph from Nazareth."

That day when Philip urged Nathanael to come and see for himself, Nathanael had a choice to make. He couldn't believe anything good could possibly come from Nazareth. He had a bigoted ideology that nothing good could possibly come out of that town. Had Nathanael stuck with his beliefs, he would have never experienced Jesus. What he came to realize was, "Jesus sees us when we think no one cares." Nathanael experienced the supernatural knowledge of the Living God.

Philip was a true friend to Nathanael. Nathanael raised valid arguments, but instead of standing in the dirt covered path bantering back and forth, Philip said, "Come and see." So often we don't know what to say when people question us about the Lord. We just need to do what Philip did, simply point them to Jesus and encourage them to check Him out for themselves.

Jesus saw Nathanael before He ever met him physically. Jesus showed Nathanael His supernatural knowledge of him. Jesus knew him completely. He knew all about Nathanael's hopes, dreams and desires. Jesus proved he was able to perceive and discern the truthfulness of Nathanael's heart.

Nathanael had an experience with Jesus. He had finally found a Rabbi who knew all. Surely, this was the Son of God. This Rabbi would teach Nathanael on a whole new level. Jesus met Nathanael right at the place of his heart's desire. Nathanael's name means, "God has given." God gave Nathanael an encounter with His Son.

Jesus saw Nathanael before He ever met him. Nathanael's response to Jesus was based off this encounter. He went one step deeper than any of the others. "You are the Son of God – the King of Israel!" Nathanael recognized the Spirit of God rested on this man who contained supernatural knowledge.

I have been where Nathanael was. I have also searched out a real relationship with my Lord. I was tired of a dull religion. I call myself a Christian, but my faith is of no value if I don't have a vibrant relationship with the Living God of the universe. Philip once told Nathanael, "Come and see for yourself." The same holds true for us. We have to experience Jesus on a one-to-one basis. We have to let go of all our preconceived notions on what He should do in our lives or how to act on our behalf.

Christianity is an individual relationship with the Son of God. We cannot experience Jesus based on what everyone else tells us. When we come to Him we too will realize, "He is the God who sees us wherever we are." He is the God who knows whatever heartache we have inside of us. Our facades cannot hide the truth of our hearts from Him.

Jesus' knowledge of Nathanael caused him to exclaim, "Rabbi, you are the Son of God – the King of Israel," John 1:49 NLT. Nathanael was the first disciple to recognize the divinity of Jesus. That was a huge step for this son of Israel. When we each come to the acknowledgement that Jesus knows us, we too will call Him, "Son of God."

A slave by the name of Hagar called God, "El Roi. He is the God who sees me." Hagar was desperate. She had just escaped abuse by her mistress. She ran away into the desert; she cried; she was sure she was alone in this world. An angel of God found her beside a spring and spoke a future over her and her son.

"She answered GOD by name, praying to the God who spoke to her, "You're the God who sees me? Yes! He saw me; and then I saw him!" Genesis 16:13 Message Bible.

God sees us. He sees us when we are lonely. He sees us when we are frightened. He sees us when we are hopeless. He sees us when we are searching for Him. Nathanael experienced this characteristic of God the day he met Jesus Christ, Son of God, Son of Man. Nathanael's story was once my story.

God knows our greatest need. We need communion with Him. It is how we are created. God knit into our souls a desire to know Him and have a relationship with Him. It is why He sent His only Son. Jesus calls us to follow Him. He knows our name and He sees our heart's desires and dreams.

Dreaming of Messiah

Nathanael escaped the heat and the legalistic restrictions of his religion. He found solace that early morning as he hid himself under the shade of a fig tree. He pursued Yahweh and not the rules of the Pharisees. He was praying for a true Rabbi, a truthful teacher to come and instruct him in the righteous ways of his religion.

He was tired of all the rules the Pharisees tacked onto the laws of Moses. In his heart he knew this type of religion could not have been Yahweh's intent. The restrictions of the Pharisees and Sadducees made worshiping God an impossible checklist for the people of Israel. Who could possibly keep up with all their addendums? Theirs was now a religion of works and not of faith. The Jewish faith had now become a religion with no hope. He gave full vent to his frustrations as he fixed his thoughts on God. He needed and longed for truth. His search for justice was a relief from these oppressive religious practices.

As he saw his friend Philip approaching, he noticed a buoyancy in Philip's steps, and a lightness to his countenance that had not been there in quite a while. "He has found something of great value," Nathanael thought to himself.

Philip could hardly contain himself as he rushed to Nathanael. His words came pouring out, "We have found the One Moses wrote about in the law. Jesus of Nazareth, the son of Joseph." Nathanael's bigotry almost excluded him from meeting the person he had been searching for. "Nazareth! Can anything good come from there?"

Curiosity sent Nathanael looking. He had to see why Philip was so adamant that this was the One about whom Moses wrote. As he approached Jesus he heard these words spoken to him, "Here is a true Israelite, in whom there is nothing false,"

Okay, that stumped him. He would continue on with his questioning. Who was this Man who now stands before him? Nathanael asked, "How do you know me?" Jesus, Son of God, answered, "I saw you while you were still under the fig tree before Philip called you."

Then Nathanael declared, "Rabbi, you are the Son of God; you are the King of Israel."

Waypoints on the way to your destination:

What was Nathanael's initial reaction to Philip's declaration?

What beliefs do you harbor that keep you from seeing Jesus in your life?

What did Philip encourage Nathanael to do?

What did Jesus tell Nathanael?

"Lord, I want a true relationship with You. Jesus I believe You are the Son of God. Come be King of my life."

The Stairway to Heaven

Day Seventeen

"Jesus asked him, "Do you believe this just because I told you I had seen you under the fig tree? You will see greater things than this." Then he said, "I tell you the truth, you will all see heaven open and the angels of God going up and down on the Son of Man, the one who is the stairway between heaven and earth" John 1:50-51 NLT.

Jesus stands before Andrew, Simon, John, James, Philip and now Nathanael. They are following along behind him. They have become a band of brothers. His words and provocative teachings hold them in rapt attention. Jesus declares to them, "You will see greater things than this. You will see heaven opened."

The prophet Isaiah once cried out to God in Isaiah 64 out of the NIV, "Oh, that You would rend the heavens and come down." We long for our Emmanuel, God with us. It is how we are made. Isaiah craved it. I crave it. Nathanael desired it. Then God comes along and does it. God answered Isaiah's plea. When Jesus came up out of the baptismal water, he looked up at the sky and saw the heavens opened and the Spirit of God descend on Him in the form of a dove. God rolled back the sky. He created a hole in the atmosphere above. Jesus, Son of God came down to us!

I am a product of the 70's. I graduated in 1979. The rock band "Led Zeppelin" released a song called, "Stairway to Heaven" in 1971. If you were in high school any time during the 70's, your prom theme or your class song might have been "Stairway to Heaven." People through the ages have been searching for that stairway. This song describes a lady who tries to buy her stairway to heaven. There is an inbred desire in each of us to find that stairway. We are searching for our Zen place. Before we were ever born God planted eternity inside each heart, and that is what every man, woman and child is searching for. We think we can attain this gift on our own. It doesn't work like that.

Psalm 78:23-24 talks of a time when God commanded the clouds to separate and He opened up the doors of heaven, then He rained down manna for the hungry Israelites to eat. They ate from heaven's grain.

I wonder what this might have looked like under the Hubble telescope. The camera placed inside this telescope has captured breathtaking anomalies throughout the heavens above us. Jesus said we would see greater things. What would we have seen the day the clouds separated, and God's hand released His Spirit to remain on Jesus?

"You will see greater things..." "You will see heaven opened..." We as created beings long to see the miraculous, the awe inspiring, the jaw dropping, and the spectacular. It is why we love magic shows and the Cirque de Sole. We want to experience shock and awe. There has to be more than the ordinary. Everyday mundane life of peat and repeat bores us.

We search for the greater things. Jesus knows this about us, because He created us and placed inside of us this longing. He created these six that stood before Him that day. He knew the desires of their hearts. They were the same as us. God placed eternity in them, and God placed eternity in us because eternity is what sends us looking for more. There is that great vacuum hole in our souls that can only be filled with the greater things. Jesus is that greater that fills us.

Jesus is the fulfillment of the cry of Isaiah's heart. Jesus did rend the heavens and come down. The rocks and the mountains did quake before Him on the day He hung on a cursed tree and breathed His last breath. Jesus is Emmanuel, God with us.

On that day standing in the middle of the road that stretched from the Jordan to Galilee, God, Yahweh, their Creator stood before these six. He was God with them, before them, standing beside them and going ahead of them. He was and still is the Greater that all of mankind is searching for. He is the eternity seed striving to blossom in our lives. Just like Isaiah cried, "Open up the heavens and come down," we all long for the One who created us to come down and nourish our dry parched souls.

He stood before them that day explaining who they were looking at. Jesus told them He was the stairway that allows mankind, His creation, to climb up and be with God. Jesus is our link back to the One who created us, and there is no other stairway, ladder, or bridge. Jesus is the stairway that leads to the very Throne Room of God.

Science has been searching for a missing link to bridge the evolutionary split between humans and other primates. Mankind has an ingrain need to know our origin. Jesus was telling His new friends, "I am that missing link."

We came into being by God. "In the beginning the Word already existed. The Word was with God and the Word was God. He existed in the beginning with God. God created everything through him, and nothing was created except through him" John 1:3 NLT. We were created through Jesus, by Jesus, and for Jesus. Those are the truths many are searching for. Some in the scientific world have a hard time recognizing this fact. God placed eternity inside of every human heart and that is why we search for greater things.

Jesus said, "You will see the heavens open..." Heaven did open up once before as Jesus came up out of the baptismal waters of the Jordan River. It will happen again. "It is written: "As surely as I live," says the Lord, "every knee will bow before me; every tongue will acknowledge God" Romans 14:11 NIV. "And the sky rolled up like a scroll and finished, and every mountain and island was dislodged from its place" Revelation 6:14 AMP. We will see this again one day. It has happened before. It will happen again. Are you ready for that day? Have you acknowledged and accepted what is inside you and what you are searching for? Eternity has been placed in your heart. Have you heard its calling?

The Miraculous Staircase

Polemistis stood in awe watching the Carpenter craft the miraculous staircase. No nails were used on the elegant stairway. Roman spikes were driven through each rung. The sound of the clanging metal being driven into the beautiful stairway made Polemistis cringe as the heavy hammer beat against the metal pegs. The mighty angel was mesmerized by the ease of the Craftsman as He swung the mallet. The degree of difficulty was apparent in this sturdy staircase. There were no support beams; none were needed. The Carpenter knew what He was doing. The sweat of His brow would hold this stairwell together.

Blood appeared to drip from His brow as He laid the hammer down. Polemistis called other warrior angels to come and see the miraculous staircase. The bottom step touched a dry dusty hill. Three crosses stood silhouetted against the setting sun. As the stairway circled its way upward, every angel gasped when they observed that the final landing wove into the very Throne Room of God Most High.

"It is finished," spoke the Carpenter. He untied His carpentry belt and picked up His double edged sword. The Commander in Chief of the Angel Armies commanded Polemistis and the Warrior Angels. "You may now ascend and descend this stairway. It is sturdy enough. It was built upon The Rock. My Son created it. This stairway bridges the gap of the great chasm that separates My creation from Me. My Son is the Miraculous Stairway that leads to My Throne Room.

Waypoints to your destination:

Do you long for more than the ordinary?

Have you searched for the miraculous?

Do you wonder about life after death?

Can you hear eternity crying out to you?

"Lord, let the cry of my heart be as Isaiah's once was. Open up the heavens and come down. Jesus I thank you that you still are Emmanuel – God with us."

The Invited Guest

Day Eighteen

"On the third day a wedding took place at Cana in Galilee. Jesus' mother was there, and Jesus and his disciples had also been invited to the wedding. When the wine was gone, Jesus' mother said to Him, "They have no more wine." "Woman why do you involve me?" Jesus replied. "My hour has not yet come." His mother said to the servants, "Do whatever he tells you" John 2:1-5 NIV.

I really appreciate that John decides to write about this wedding. I think too often we picture Jesus as a stoic philosopher who did not know how to kick up His heels. At times, I feel Christianity has painted Him as a grim faced servant. Though He did come to seek and to serve, Jesus was more than that. Our Savior was a multifaceted personality. We must quit domesticating who He really was. Jesus was not the domicile wall flower some people believe Him to be. Christianity has in the past tried to soften His edges, trying to make His puzzle piece fit into our comprehension of who He needs to be in our society. This ruins the picture of Jesus' true character.

Jesus commanded the room when He entered. His charismatic personality could not be ignored. Jesus did not get lost in the crowd. Jaws dropped the moment He began to speak. Jesus unique presence entered a wedding celebration, and changed the whole outcome of the event. What could have been a disastrous and embarrassing moment for a happy couple, was changed into jubilee because Jesus turned H2O into wine. Thousands of years later, we still speak of the impact He made by just being present at this wedding.

Our Savior celebrated and embraced life. He was the Kodak moment when He accepted social invitations. A Jewish wedding was a time of celebration and feasting, where the happy couple invited friends and family to come, eat, drink, dance, and be merry. This unknown couple in John 2 invited Jesus to attend their celebration, Jesus went where He was invited, and He brought His new friends to celebrate.

His mom was also present. Jesus was part of an earthly family. He was just coming into His public ministry, but He still had time for His dear mom. I am a mom so I appreciate this scene. I love celebrating with my kids and their families. Celebrations are part of life. Jesus went to a wedding with His mom. I smile at the picture that paints.

At the moment of this wedding, Jesus had not yet performed a miracle. He was not well known because He had just arrived into the area with His buddies. The invite to the wedding probably came because of His mother. The couple may have been related to Mary or were close family friends.

A Jewish wedding feast lasted a week. The groom was responsible for making sure there were adequate provisions. This included having enough wine for all the guests for the entire seven days. It would have been a social faux pas had they run out of food or wine. In fact the family could actually have been fined.

Jesus' mother, Mary, may have been a type of wedding coordinator for this event, running behind the scenes making sure everything was going smoothly. That was most likely the reason she knew the wine was running out. An embarrassing social moment was about to happen which would have left an indelible black mark on the happy couple's reputation for years to come. Mary knew there was an invited guest among them who could change this outcome. She knew who Her Son was, and she knew what her Son could do. As she scurried behind the scenes, Mary was not about to allow humiliation dampen this couple's joyous occasion.

She had first-handedly witnessed Jesus growing in wisdom and stature with both God and man. She had seen Him surprise the Pharisees and the teachers with His wisdom and knowledge though He was but twelve years old. She knew this man named Jesus. He had been her Son now for thirty years. She had called Him, "Child." She had a love relationship with Him before He ever performed one miracle. So she called on Him now.

There had to have been a tone in their exchange that we are not privy to these thousands of years later. We can read the words but their tone cannot be inflected onto the page. We have to add it. That is why I read Jesus' reply with playful teasing. Otherwise, how could we go on with Mary's instructions to the servants, "Do whatever He tells you." Jesus never agreed to Mary's request. We may even read negativity into His response. When, Jesus asked, "Why do you involve me?" Mary translated it "Ok. I will do what you wish." Their banter was, "This is what you said, but this is what you meant," type of dialogue. Because of their love relationship, Mary knew Jesus would respond positively to her request.

Some may find Jesus' reply to his mother as shocking, and depending on your tone when you read verse 4, I can see how you might perceive it as such. I have a different perception though. I am a mother of a son. When I read Jesus' and Mary's banter, a smile comes to my lips. You see there was a time my son would playfully rib me and call me, "Woman". Now mind you, I didn't always find this salutation as an endearing response from my son. In fact at times the term would flat out wear on my last good nerve. I must confess, I have exploded and surprised Landry with the force of my anger as he addressed me "Woman."

But now... Those memories bring back good times. I smile and quite truthfully I miss that term of endearment from my son. It is the way we worked. He would needle me, pushing me to a near breaking point and I soon learned to show no weakness. I got used to this salutation because I realized that he was really saying, "Mom, I love you." This was the way we were with each other. It was the way our relationship worked. He would tease and I would give right back because we love each other and we trust each other. I know Landry respects me and if it is in his power, he will always respond to my requests.

My two daughters never called me "Woman." I don't think it is in their DNA make up. They call me "Mom" and I respond. Different types of relationships but each with the same amount of love written into them. My mother/daughter relationships aren't built around the teasing banter. We operate differently, just as my brother and I operate differently with my own mother. As I sit and reflect on their relationship, I see the same thing going on. I remember the ease with which my brother used to tease and goad my mother.

Mother's and son's relationships just work on teasing playfulness. My own husband has a way with his mom that his two sisters would never try. He tells her and encourages her to try new things. He pushes her to go past her comfort zones.

My daughter has two sons. There is just a way they treat their mom that is different compared to their dad. The amount of love is the same in each relationship but the care and input is different. With their dad, it's all rough and rowdy. They climb, wrestle, and tackle their dad, but they hold their mother in high esteem. Now, my baby boy has a baby boy of his own. This boy will also have a different relationship with Landry than he does with his mommy. Different types of relationships with same amount of love written into the cadence of each DNA.

This is what I think about as I read Jesus' words, "Woman, why do you involve me?" I hear my own son playfully call me "Woman." The Greek text reads, "Dear Lady." Dear Lady. He was calling her a term of honor. Mary was a lady in every sense of the word. The definition of lady is – a woman of superior social position. It denotes a woman to whom homage or obedience is due. There had been a season in Mary's life where there were whisperings and innuendos circling about her character. Many must have tried to count the months between her marriage to Joseph and the birth of her first born son, Jesus. She had risen above all that slanderous garbage and now she was a woman with a mission.

I think that is one of the reasons I love Jesus so much. He had a dry sense of humor, and a charismatic way about Him. He makes me smile as I read His conversations with people. There was a bantering of back and forth with those who plunged into dialogue with Him. Their conversations stirred the mind. He didn't resent their requests or their interruptions. Jesus welcomed them, and more often than not His reply and response was a test of their endurance and persistence in their need.

I wonder if that is what He is doing with His own mother in this situation? I think He knew He was about to perform His first miracle. I think He had gotten the go ahead from His Father. I think He even knew how He was going to create wine from water. I think His response to Mary was just His way of stimulating and activating her faith in Him. That is what I think. What do you think?

No one will ever have a mother/son relationship with Jesus. That position was filled long ago, but we can have a different type of love relationship with Him. He calls us friends. He calls us family. He calls us loved, and He tells us come with persistence. We are to approach Him with our every need and don't give up. Because of His great love for us, He wants to fill our stone jars with the new wine of His blessings.

The Celebration

Chathan and Hannah smashed the kiddish cup after drinking the wine of blessing. They were lifted up and carried under the chuppah. The canopy twirled in sequence with the bride and groom as they were spun in the air, and carried around by the groomsmen. "Let the celebrating begin," announced the host. Everything had been prepared. The food and wine had been bought. It was enough to last seven days. The invitations had been sent. The guests had arrived with great anticipation for this wedding celebration.

The dance began. The feast was spread before the guests, and the stone jars had been filled with red wine. The guests clapped, danced, and sang as they twirled Chathan and Hannah in exhilarating glee. The festivities had been going on for several days now. Chathan hadn't given thought to the wine nor food on hand. He knew Mary had it under control. She had been a godsend.

The well-wishers twirled him again. He caught sight of Mary's Son. Chathan was glad he had invited Jesus and His friends. Jesus had carried the party. His presence was magnifying. His countenance drew in every person. Chathan had observed Him these past few days. There was a certain aura about this man. Jesus' physical appearance was as any other man's. Nothing really stood out. It was simply that being in His presence a person felt wanted and cherished. When Jesus was engaged in conversation, you could tell He was present in the moment. He made every guest feel comfortable. Jesus knew how to make everyone feel important and as if they mattered.

He smiled when he saw Jesus and Mary deep in conversation. Mother and Son. They were comfortable with each other. Chathan could tell they were talking matters of importance, and it concerned him. Then he looked into Mary's confident eyes, and with a wave of her hand, servants were summoned. She was directing once again. He could tell she had matters well under hand. Jesus then spoke to the servants and pointed to the stone jars. "All things were under control," Chathan comforted himself with this knowledge. This guest named Jesus could handle whatever disturbance this feast may bring.

Waypoints to your destination:

How would you label your relationship with Jesus – family, friend, acquaintance, or indifferent?

What disruption are you currently experiencing that need the changing touch of Jesus?

What is your first response to Mary and Jesus' dialogue?

What life event do you need to invite Jesus to?

Lord Jesus, I invite you into every part of my life, the celebrations and the storms. Change my water into Your wine of blessing.

His Way

Day Nineteen

The wine supply ran out during the festivities, so Jesus' mother told him "They have no more wine." "Dear woman, that's not our problem," Jesus replied. "My time has not yet come." But his mother told the servants, "Do whatever He tells you" John 2:3-5 NLT.

There is a hymn that is hard for me to just go all in. It's called "Have Thine Own Way" by Adelaide Pollard. The first few lines are, "Have thine own way, Lord! Have thine own way. Thou art the potter, I am the clay. Mould me and make me after thy will, while I am waiting yielded and still."

Adelaide Pollard penned the words to this famous hymn during a time when Miss Pollard was trying to raise funds to make a trip to Africa and serve as a missionary there. She was unsuccessful. She had her life planned out and it wasn't going according to her plan. She heard the prayer, "It really doesn't matter what you do with us, Lord – just have your way with our lives..." Miss Pollard didn't make it to Africa at this time. Instead she went home and wrote this beloved hymn, "Have Thine own way." Are you humming that familiar hymn now? I am, but instead of singing the words from memory, I am concentrating on their meaning. "Mold me and make me after thy will" The words don't say, "Lord, this is what I want to do now make it happen." This hymn was inspired by a simple prayer of an elderly woman at a prayer meeting. Miss Pollard heard this woman pray, "It really doesn't matter what you do with us, Lord – just have your way with our lives..." I think of this type of submission to God's will, as I read John 2:1-11 and the story of Jesus changing water into wine.

Nowhere do you read in these verses that Mary told Jesus what to do or how to fix this problem. Mary simply reported the disruptive issue. Mary's words to the servants reveal that she was willing to let her Son do whatever He pleased. She trusted His path. Mary knew Jesus would do what was right.

It's such a hard principle to yield to, isn't it? I want to control my future. I want to be in charge of my destiny. It is really difficult to yield to the Lord's will. I want to steer the rudders of my own ship, and be my own captain. I want to be in charge and go where I want to go, watch what I want to watch, and be friends with whom I wish. That is what I want.

"Captain O Captain." I want to navigate my own ship. I want to steer clear of turbulent waters. I don't want Jesus to take the wheel. Even though I can't ride or steer a horse to save my life, I don't want to hand over the reigns to the One who controls all of nature. Inside of me lurks a control freak. I want to take charge of the situation at hand and tell Jesus the best way to handle it. However, as I contemplate Mary's example here, she yielded. She simply brought the problem to Jesus and left it in his hands.

The prophet, Isaiah, made several comparisons to the nation Israel being like clay in The Potter's hands. "Yet you, Lord, are our Father. We are the clay, you are the potter; we are all the work of your hand," Isaiah 64:8 NIV. "Woe to those who quarrel with their Maker, those who are nothing but potsherds among the potsherds on the ground. Does the clay say to the potter, 'What are you making?' Does your work say, 'The potter has no hands?' Isaiah 45:9 NIV.

Have you ever told Jesus how He needs to fix this situation you are in? I have! Have you ever thought you gave your problem to Jesus but then later returned and picked it up again so that you can fix it yourself? I have!

We need to learn from Mary's example. She simply reported the dilemma and then told the servants, "Do whatever He tells you." She exited the stage pointing to her Son. There is only one right answer for every problem you face. "Point others to Jesus."

Because an elderly woman once prayed: "It really doesn't matter what you do with us, Lord – just have your way with our lives..." Sometimes our lives don't turn out as we planned. Can you pray, "Just have Your Own Way"?

What He Says

Dulous approached the regal matron, "Madam, that was the last of the wine." Mary paused for a moment regarding this faithful steward. She took a deep breath and mentally composed her reply. "It will be taken care of," she assured the worried servant.

Her eyes flew to her Son standing next to the cleaning pots. Jesus stood so confidently among the wedding guests. His new friends were enjoying themselves at this jubilant event. The entourage moved freely through the crowd. Jesus laughed with abandonment as he listened intently to the stories of the wedding guests.

Mary knew what she must do and who she must ask. She hadn't a clue how Jesus would rectify this potentially embarrassing faux pas, but she was confident He could. More than that, she was confident He would, and she boldly walked up to her Son. Her hand tugged at His elbow, then she pulled Him aside. "They have run out of wine," Mary confided. She smiled at His reply, and turned to Dulous, "Whatever He says to you, do it."

Then Mary strode off. She wanted to enjoy and celebrate also, and with that problem placed in the proper hands, she could do just that.

Waypoints to your destination:

What situation are you facing that is difficult to find a solution for?

What did Mary do when she found out about the predicament and what did she tell the servants to do?

Have you ever told Jesus how He must solve your problem?

How hard is it to say, "Have thine own way, Lord?

Lord, Your way is best. God help me to give it all to You and leave it there. I'm tired of going back and picking it up. Lord, help me to trust You and let You handle things Your way.

The Broken Road

Day Twenty

"Now six stone water jars had been set there for Jewish purification. Each contained 20 or 30 gallons. 'Fill the jars with water,' Jesus told them. So they filled them to the brim. Then He said to them, 'Now draw some out and take it to the chief servant.' And they did," John 2:6-7 HCSB.

Two years ago I sat down once again on my piano bench. I hadn't touched the piano for at least forty-four years. At age 54, I decided this time I would conquer this thing. I was going to play the piano beautifully even if I had to practice all day. I think I got to page 21 in my new piano lesson book, "Learning to play the piano for dummies." I could play, "Twinkle Twinkle Little Star," quite eloquently. In fact it made my mom cry. After all those years of fighting with me to practice, I was finally sitting down to learn to play the piano when I was well past middle age.

I think my downfall came when I became too boastful with my skills and decided to learn Chopin's "Prelude in D" just so I could impress my grandson. I soon learned my problem was not in my desire. I had all the desire in the world to sit at a piano and produce beautiful music to echo off the ivories. I have an issue coordinating my left hand to play the bass clef and my right hand to play different keys and different tempos on the treble clef. My problem was I am the clay and I was trying to tell the Potter what I wanted to be molded into. I wanted to become a great concert pianist at age 54, or at the very least I would like to play, "O Come all Ye Faithful" at Christmas time with all my family coming around the piano and singing Christmas Carols while they ooh and ah over my piano skills.

"What sorrow awaits those who argue with their Creator. Does a clay pot argue with its maker? Does the clay dispute with the one who shapes it, saying, 'Stop, you're doing it wrong!' does the pot exclaim, 'How clumsy can you be?'" Isaiah 45:9 NLT

"O Israel, can I not do to you as this potter has done to his clay? As the clay is in the potter's hand, so are you in my hand" Jeremiah 18:6 NLT.

"And yet, O Lord, you are our Father. We are the clay, and you are the potter. We all are formed by your hand" Isaiah 64:8 NLT.

I don't know why, but as I read these verses, I think of the green lump of clay some animator formed into a body and a television Claymation figure emerged. My generation knew him as Gumby. Gumby had a horse named Pokey. Pokey was fashioned from a brown lump of clay. Pokey and Gumby hit the airways in 1956 on the Howdy Doody Show. Do you think as that clay animator stared at that green rectangle shaped clay, he heard the clay speak to him? Did that green clay say, "Make me into a strange shaped clay boy?" No, Gumby was molded by Art Clokey. Gumby became Claymation because Art had an imagination that dreamed up this strange green clay boy.

"Then the Lord God formed a man from the dust of the ground and breathed into his nostrils the breath of life, and the man became a living being" Genesis 2:7 NLT

I wanted to play the piano like a concert pianist. I want to make beautiful music unto the Lord, but for the life of me I can't sing or play in key. My musical abilities are like the broken C key on my piano keyboard that just sticks there and the only sound emanating from the broken key is a flat hollow sound. So I come to a different keyboard, my computer keyboard, and I start writing and reflecting on certain passages of scripture, and when I don't see how the Potter can possibly mold this brokenness into a decorative vessel, I begin to write and see the jar He is molding me into.

"But who are you, a human being to talk back to God? 'Shall what is formed say to the one who formed, 'Why did you make me like this?'" Does not the potter have the right to make out of the same lump of clay some pottery for special purposes and some for common use?" Romans 9:20-21 NIV.

Every single one of us are created by a Master Artist. We are a lump of clay thrown onto the Potter's Wheel. From His imagination we are formed into some type of pottery. Some of us are created to plant flowers in, some are made to pour water into, and some are used in ordinary everyday life. I don't know your shape. I can't concentrate or worry about what you will become. I have to concentrate on what the Potter is creating me to be. I must stay pliable moldable clay. The Potter's hands will get messy as He turns this clay on His wheel. He will have to use water to keep this clay moldable. I am not finished yet. I am a work in progress. We will see what I will become. However, it's a pretty safe bet you won't see me on the concert tour.

The day Jesus turned the water into wine; He saw six stone jars just sitting randomly off to the side. They weren't being used at this time. They were placed there for ceremonial cleansing according to the religious practices at the time. Did those inanimate stone vessels expect to be used to bless this wedding that day? No, as I said they are inanimate. We are like those stone pots. Jesus wants to use us. He wants to pour into us so that we can become a blessing to those around us. We just have to be made available to Jesus.

The other day my grandson gave my daughter a flowerpot that he decorated for Mother's Day. He was telling me about a mishap that occurred. One of his friend's clay pots broke as she was giving it to her mother and the dirt and the flower planted in the pot spilled all over the carpet. He said his friend was sad.

I feel like that has happened to me upon multiple occasions in my spiritual walk with the Lord. Winds and storms come and my clay pot that is filled with beautiful colorful flowers torpedoes off my porch. The ground becomes littered with my brokenness and dirt.

Did I mention that at times as the Potter is fashioning a clay vessel he must pound the clay down while he twirls it around on His wheel? As the Potter is molding the pot sometimes the pot has cracks in it. The Potter then beats the clay down so that He can reshape the vessel. Like I said, I must focus on becoming a moldable pliable vessel in the Potter's Hand.

There is a Japanese art of taking broken pottery and repairing it with lacquer dusted or mixed with powdered gold. It is called Kintsugi, and it means golden repair. The result of the mended vessels is pure genius. The vases that come from the shattered pieces are none other than breathtaking. This is what Jesus does to the broken pieces of our lives. He takes each piece and dusts it off, then glues it back together with the gold from His treasure chest. The gold He uses is the pavement of the roads in Heaven. These vessels

He creates from our brokenness become His masterpieces. Have you taken your brokenness to Him yet?

The Clay and the Potter

Yahweh approached His potter's wheel. With great care, He donned His apron. It had collected quite a bit of dirt and clay through the years, but the Potter did not mind. He cherished the memories of creating each vessel.

His gentle hand reached into the raw clay, and cupped out a handful of the red dirt. Yahweh then threw that clay onto the wheel and He began to spin. With skillful hands He molded the clay which wasn't quite pliant enough, so He beat the clay back into a lump shaped ball. The Potter began again. This time just as a vase was beginning to appear from the lump of clay; He saw a small crack beginning to grow because the clay had become to dry on the wheel. The wise Potter then threw water onto the vase and began working it again.

It was then the clay vessel spoke to the Potter, "Make me beautiful. Add some color to me. You can also throw in some of that gold You have lying over there. I want to be used in the courts of royalty. I want all the other pieces of pottery to bow down and be in awe of my exquisiteness."

The Potter frowned at this lump of clay. His thumb began to add pressure to the middle of the vase. "Stop, what are you doing? Why are You being so clumsy with me? Why are you tearing down my beautiful shape?" Cried the vase who wanted so badly to be admired by all.

Yahweh reworked the clay with all-knowing hands. What once was going to be a vessel to carry frankincense to a King, was now going to be used to wash the hands of a governor named Pilate.

Waypoints to your destination:

What did Jesus use to change water into wine?

What were His instructions to the servants?

Have you ever tried to convince God how He should take care of your business?

What does Romans 9:20-21 say about the same lump of clay in the Potter's Hand?

"Lord, it is so hard to let go and let God. Lord, work in my heart. Help me yield to the Potter's Hand. Lord, You and You alone know what is best for me. God, please make me pliable and yielding to submit to Your wisdom."

The Empty Road

Day Twenty One

"Nearby stood six stone water jars, the kind used by the Jews for ceremonial washing, each holding from twenty to thirty gallons. Jesus said to the servants, "Fill the jars with water"; so they filled them to the brim. Then he told them, "Now draw some out and take it to the master of the banquet." They did so, and the master of the banquet tasted the water that had been turned into wine. He did not realize where it had come from, though the servants who had drawn the water knew. Then he called the bridegroom aside and said, "Everyone brings out the choice wine first and then the cheaper wine after the guests have had too much to drink; but you have saved the best till now." What Jesus did here in Cana of Galilee was the first of the signs through which He revealed His glory; and His disciples believed in Him" John 2:6-11 NIV.

She loaded each child into the car. Her husband buckled their infant son in. She helped her two daughters fasten their seat belts. It was Sunday. The family of five were headed to church. "This is the day the Lord has made and I will rejoice and be glad in it." Isn't that how the song goes? She had learned it so many years ago as she sat while a little girl in Sunday school classes and learned the bible stories and the Sunday school songs. She had loved going to church and hearing the adventures of all the bible heroes. So what had happened? Where was her rejoicing? Why wasn't she glad to go to church and sing three verses to the familiar hymns? Why did her mind drift and thoughts wander to consider her duties of wife and motherhood for the rest of the week? She would often find herself nodding off during the sermons. What was wrong with her?

This faith she was practicing or more like posing felt like a noose around her neck. It was a rote habit. Six days of doing the same things over and over then waking and getting ready for Sunday. She was practicing religious habits; habits that did nothing to fill her true needs. They pulled into the church parking lot. She helped her children out of the car. She quietly pleaded, "Lord, if this is all there is to Christianity, what's the use? Am I drifting simply to live a moral life and wait for eternity? What about the abundant life You speak about in Your word?"

Does her story sound familiar to you? It does to me because at one point in my life that was my testimony. I had lived many years as a Christian. My faith was in name only. I had accepted Jesus as my Savior. I knew I had inherited a life eternal. This body would one day fade away, but I had the assurance that I would live forever with Jesus in heaven. That was the extent of my religion.

My everyday life was lived by my striving and my own self-efforts and I was living for my own selfish desires. There was no life lived abundantly. The joy and happiness was self-produced and had no roots that went down deep into my spirit to help me in times of despair and feelings of failure; failure at being a wife and failure at being a mom.

There had to be more to Christianity and way down deep in the quietness of my soul, God was gently whispering to me, "There was!" There is an abundant life for each of us who are called by His name. We are called His Children. We have been adopted as sons and daughters of the Most High God, but I was choosing not to live like a Child of God. I couldn't see the royalty of my true identity. I am a chosen person. I am part of a royal priesthood. I am a daughter of the Great I Am! And I have been given an abundant life. That is my inheritance!

That is the story of the water turned to wine. The stone water jars were used for Jewish religious practices of cleansing. They held water for external washing but they couldn't cleanse inside the soul. The religious habits couldn't cleanse the heart and bring about everlasting joy. Neither could my religious habit of making sure I was in church every Sunday. The truth is, religious habits are deficient for bringing about true life and experiencing the forgiveness of our sins.

"Jesus said to the servants, "Fill the jars with water"; so they filled them to the brim" John 2:7 NIV.

The stone water jars were empty; just like practicing a religion leaves you empty and depleted. The water in these jars had been depleted by the religious activity of trying to cleanse ourselves, but Jesus says, "Fill them with water." Only Jesus can fill our emptiness. Only Jesus can turn water and religion into true joy. Only Jesus can truly cleanse and bring forgiveness and take our sins as far as the east is from the west. Jesus brought fullness where there was emptiness, and joy where there was disappointment.

There was a problem at this wedding. They had run out of wine. The shortage of wine was relieved by Jesus' intervention. The wine is symbolic for joy. The wedding celebration was about to be halted because the joy the world offered had run out, but Jesus created something better.

"And the master of the banquet tasted the water that had been turned into wine. He did not realize where it had come from, though the servants who had drawn the water knew. Then he called the bridegroom aside and said, "Everyone brings out the choice wine first and the cheaper wine after the guests have had too much to drink; but you have saved the best till now" John 2:9-10 NIV.

The joys of this world come to an end. They have no lasting value. There is no residual to what the world offers us. Shopping sprees, overeating, worldly wealth, self-indulgence, and religious practices, all these things leave us depleted. They are an empty road, and have no power to bring true lasting joy and abundant living. Trust me I know. I have witnessed this depletion in my own life and in the lives of others. This principal is lived out on reality TV series every week on primetime television. The people who seem to have the world at their fingertips are some of the saddest emptiest people I can think of. But it can all change in the blink of an eye.

Jesus is the answer. Only Jesus can fill us with true wine, the best wine, the joy of the Lord type wine. The world offers the best at first and then, once you are hooked, things start to unravel. The life of abundance Jesus offers is continual. God wants what is best for us; we just have to train our thoughts to believe that. God wants us to enjoy the finest blessings, but there is a key to unlock these blessings. Jesus was invited to the wedding. You have to invite Jesus before You can be filled with the miracle. Before the guests at the wedding tasted the new wine, Jesus had to have been invited. There would have been no new wine if the Wine Producer had not shown up.

Jesus says, "Here I am! I stand at the door and knock. If anyone hears my voice and opens the door, I will come in and eat with that person, and they with me." Revelation 3:20 NIV.

For me to begin living the abundant, overflowing best life God has for me, I had to invite Jesus into my everyday ordinary life. The religion of Christian practices could not bring the sustenance my starving soul needed. I had to put away practices and exchange them for a vital animated relationship with the Wine Producer, so I cried out, "God I need more of You."

Filled to the Brim

Nathanael stood off to the side mesmerized at the events unfolding before him. Never in his wildest dreams did he ever believe the road he had chosen to take would lead him to this wedding miracle. He watched as this new Rabbi took over. The confidence Jesus possessed inspired Nathanael. It seemed such a minor problem. No more wine, no big deal. The wedding would be over sooner than later, but then Jesus stepped in and took over matters.

The stone jars were empty vessels that stood off to the side. Inanimate objects, ordinary objects that were placed out of the way like needless things. Out of sight, out of mind, but Jesus used them to usher in a new celebration. "Fill them to the brim," Nathanael had heard Jesus tell the servants. What once was empty, Jesus commanded to be filled, and what was once obscure objects, now became a focal point of celebration.

Nathanael could feel the fullness of joy rising in him also. A hopeless religion filled with law was beginning to be replaced with new wine. He had once sat under a tree dreaming of a true relationship with Yahweh, and now he could feel it was at hand. His feet began tapping, keeping time with the new song the band was beginning to play. The dancing began again, and this time he joined in celebrating the new song.

This Rabbi was different. This Rabbi was the Son of God.

Waypoints to your destination:

What was the description of the stone jars?

What did Jesus tell the servants to fill them with?

What did the master of ceremonies say of the new wine?

Describe a time when religion left you empty?

"Lord, in Your presence is fullness of joy. God fill me to the brim with the wine of Your Spirit. Use me as You used the stone jars."

Home Base

Day Twenty Two

"What Jesus did here in Cana of Galilee was the first of the signs through which he revealed his glory; and His disciples believed in Him. After this He went down to Capernaum with His mother and brothers and His disciples. There they stayed for a few days" John 2:11-12 NIV.

I don't know why but I love the thought of Jesus taking a road trip with His family and friends before He got too busy in public ministry. He traveled with his mother, his brothers, and his disciples from Cana to Capernaum. It was a day's walk. Capernaum was by the sea so this jaunt was about twenty-five miles down hill. A marathon is twenty-six miles, but this little traveling band wasn't running.

They were in it for the camaraderie. In companionship they went where Jesus led. This Man had just turned water into wine. A certain truth had been revealed to them at the wedding. Jesus had authority over the elements, i.e. water and wine. Jesus had captured their attention and inspired awe. Jesus' might and power manifested before them. His glory and true nature became evident to those who followed Him. When these followers beheld Jesus, it was like an open window to the height and breadth and depth of God Almighty.

Walking twenty-five miles with Jesus would become a natural occurrence for this group because the One they followed could change water into wine. They were just beginning to embark on their lifelong journey with Jesus.

They are the heroes and heroines in His Story. They are about to live a life worth living and tell a story worth telling. They had been observers of His first sign. Each miracle Jesus performed was a sermon in action. Jesus had proved to these first few that He had authority over natural elements. His disciples now believed in Him. Jesus began teaching them of His Father and His authority over all created things. We read each of these events from the backside of His Story, but for these new disciples each day and every new event brought marvels that were difficult to understand.

Their thoughts had to be swirling as they walked downhill to Capernaum discussing the wedding with each other and with Jesus. This was His entourage. Did they have butterflies as they talked amongst themselves? Surely they couldn't let go of the miracle they had just witnessed. Now they were following the Man who could make things happen. They were about to make memories that would sustain them for the turbulence that was to come.

Jesus knew what lay ahead for them. The days would be long. The ministry would be draining for them, so He took them to a seaside village. He was going to establish a home base for them. It was their command center. Every military mission begins by establishing a command center on the outskirts of enemy territory. Capernaum became their home base. Ever play hide and seek before? The first thing you do is establish a base. It's the safe place you run to when you are being chased. Jesus knew He would be sending this group behind enemy lines so He established a place of origin. It was the home they would return to after a mission.

Before this group would ever begin acts of service, Jesus served them at home in His presence. Jesus was intentional in everything He did, and He intentionally took this group down to Capernaum so that they could experience a new awareness of God's Presence. Jesus was, is, and will always be Emmanuel, God with us.

God was now manifested in their world and they had to gain knowledge of this. They needed time to wrap their minds around the enormity of who He really was. They would eat, drink and relax while He spoke and taught.

It was homeschooling 101, and Capernaum was their home base. It was here that they began their lessons of who Jesus was. They gained a truer perspective of what it meant that Emmanuel had come into their world. At Capernaum, Jesus revealed who He truly was. Before they would ever begin this "new norm" of public ministry, they had to reframe what everyday life would look like from this day forward.

In essence they were on a retreat with Jesus as the master teacher. However, the word retreat also carries with it a negative connotation in battle terms. No commander wants to issue a retreat. It is a command to pull back and allows the enemy to gain territory, but in Jesus' wisdom that was the beginning of His plan of attack. He took this group on a retreat so that they could get into a frame of mind to trust Him, rely on Him, and adhere to Him, and to go where He led them.

Capernaum was a seaside metropolis located on the banks of the Sea of Galilee. The traffic of the world passed through Capernaum. It was the port that led to everywhere. If location is key to real estate, then Jesus couldn't have chosen a better place to establish His command center. The greatest roads of the ancient world passed through Galilee.

The gospel of Matthew clarifies Jesus' decision to set up camp at Capernaum. Matthew 4:13-16 explains this was to fulfill the prophecy of Isaiah. Again, Jesus was never haphazard in His decision making process. Everything He did was in accordance with God's plan that had been laid out from before the time of creation. Jesus gave His followers a firm foundation from which they would go out into all the world.

Home base, command central, and war rooms, the military begins each mission from this location. Jesus established a home base before He sent His soldiers behind the enemy's lines.

We have been given our home base also. We are fighting in hostile territory. Our enemy prowls around like a roaring lion, but our Commander-In-Chief left an empty tomb for us to fight from. It was where He waved His victory flag over death, hell and the grave. We fight from a place a victory. The empty tomb is our command center.

Behind the Lines

The field general set up base camp. The Son of God rolled out the terrain maps. He knew His enemy well. The battle had been raging before these mountains had been formed. This region had been shrouded in darkness for far too long. His Father had shown Him the shadow lands of death.

"There. Set up Your base camp at Capernaum. Those whom You will send out need a home to return to. You will meet with them there. Your disciples will regroup with You after each mission. This is the place I have ordained. These people have been walking in darkness, but no more. You will supply them with Your light. Take back the ground the enemy has stolen," His Father commanded as He gave Jesus these plans. Jesus obeyed.

Jesus led His followers down the road called "Via Maris" (the Way of the Sea). It was heavily traveled. You could tell by the ruts the trader caravans had carved into the highway. Many in His group were heading toward home, Simon included. Jesus could tell they were excited.

He still caught their stares of amazement. When they thought He wasn't listening, He heard their murmurs of wonder. "Did you see the water become wine right before our eyes? One moment it was clear liquid and the next the deep red burgundy from the color of the choicest wines in all of Israel!" Jesus heard their whisperings.

In humility to His Father He prayed, "Father thank you for the authority You gave me. Now a spark of belief has been lit in their thoughts. Be with us as we set up home base."

The matted hair on the back of Apollyon's neck bristled. He heard what sounded like a Roman Legion traversing into his shadow lands. He snaked his way to peer over the cliff above the sea. Vile oozed from every spore. Jesus was establishing a command center in Apollyon's territory. His fog of evil had shrouded the land of Zebulun and Naphtali for centuries. Now the Glory of the Lord God Almighty was penetrating his darkness.

Apollyon wasn't omniscient. His only tactic was to hold on and wait for an opportune time to attack. He would use the Pharisees and their pompous set of religious laws. He would enchant with betrayal, and He would turn one of these men into a traitor for his cause.

Waypoints on the way to your destination:

What did the miracle of turning water into wine accomplish?

What does John 2:11 say the disciples did after this sign?

Where did the entourage go after leaving Cana?

What are your thoughts about Jesus setting up a home base for His followers?

"Lord, thank you for Your protection. Heaven is our final home. We are only travelers traversing through this world, but while we journey, we thank You for the empty tomb and the victory it contains."

On the Road Again

Day Twenty Three

"It was nearly time for the Jewish Passover celebration so Jesus went to Jerusalem. In the Temple area He saw merchants selling cattle, sheep and doves for sacrifices; He also saw dealers at tables exchanging foreign money. Jesus made a whip from some ropes and chased them all out of the Temple He drove out the sheep and cattle, scattered the money changers' coins over the floor, and turned over their tables. Then, going over to the people who sold doves, He told them, "Get these things out of here. Stop turning my Father's house into a marketplace!" Then His disciples remembered this prophecy from the Scriptures: "Passion for God's house will consume me" John 2:13-16 NLT.

After setting up command centers and base camps, the missions begin. Generals send out the troops and the battles ensue. Blood is spilled and soldiers are wounded. It is the circle of war.

Spiritual retreats and times spent with Jesus are refreshing, but you must come down from the mountain top at some time. Life still carries on. All good things must come to an end. Jesus and His followers couldn't stay by the tranquil sea forever. They had to go out into the world and engage.

Real life was calling. The Jewish Passover was approaching. Jesus left the serenity of the Sea of Galilee, and headed to Jerusalem to fulfill the requirement of the Law that He had given Moses once upon a mountaintop.

136

"Jesus said, 'Don't misunderstand why I have come. I did not come to abolish the law of Moses or the writings of the prophets. No, I came to accomplish their purpose" Matthew 5:17 NLT.

"Three times a year all your men must appear before the Lord your God at the place He will choose: at the Festival of Unleavened Bread, the Festival of Weeks and the Festival of Tabernacles. No one should appear before the LORD empty-handed" Deuteronomy 16:16 NIV.

It wasn't His first trip to Jerusalem. Jesus would have crisscrossed this land multiple times, because He came to fulfill the law. Jesus traveled to Jerusalem at least three times a year for the Festival of Unleavened Bread, the Festival of Weeks and the Festival of Tabernacles.

The Festival of Unleavened Bread began the eve after Passover celebration. So, the group left their home in Capernaum and headed to the busy city of Jerusalem joining the throngs of other pilgrims and worshippers who were set to take part in the annual Passover feast.

It was 85 miles to the Temple in Jerusalem. The terrain's dramatic elevation changes were one of the perils of this pilgrimage. The land across the Jordan was a land of mountains and valleys. There were no paved roads, no cars, and no bicycles. The least expensive mode of transportation was by foot, so they cinched up their sandals and headed out for their hike.

Did Jesus ever get exhausted as he traversed back and forth across the Jordan? Did his legs and and thighs burn as he traipsed up and down the hills of Judea?

They were a ragtag group that followed this Rabbi from Galilee. Most were fisherman and blue collar workers. None had graduated from seminary, but they had caught a glimpse of Jesus' power and authority so they would climb any mountain He did.

The capitol city of Jerusalem loomed before them. The entirety of the Temple Mount rose as a massive white polished marble structure beckoning to weary travelers to come in awe. Herod the Great had recently rebuilt this Temple. Gold gleamed above gates and entrances. Off to the side of the beautiful city a rocky unattractive hill was lined with Roman crosses. These were the instruments used for the death penalty for all who rose against Rome. It was called Golgotha. Not far from it were tombs cut into the rock. These tombs housed the decaying bodies of the dead. The travelers would have passed by this hill.

As Jesus entered the city it would have been hustling and bustling with worshippers from all over Israel. Roman soldiers stood stoically posted watching and observing, guarding against riots and outbreaks from such a huge crowd.

Eighteen years before, at the age of 12, Jesus had sat in these very temple courts. "After three days they found Him in the temple courts, sitting among the teachers, listening to them and asking them questions. Everyone who heard Him was amazed at His understanding and His answers" Luke 2:47 NIV. Probably many of those same teachers were still among the group who sat in the temple courts on this day.

Today as Jesus climbed the Temple steps the sound of raucous behavior and dishonest trading invaded His heart. The Temple courts were no longer filled with sincere worshipers, but they were littered with the riffraff of money changers and dishonest merchants who disrespected the House of God. They were feeding off the naivety of the innocent pilgrims.

Jesus entered stage right. He climbed each step leading up to His Father's House. The thievery and conniving at the Temple courts shredded the Holy moments. He led the way for this band of brothers. Andrew, Simon, John, James, Philip, and Nathanael climbed the steps behind Him. Jesus had come to the Temple to honor His Father and to pray, but what He found appalled and infuriated Him. His passion and zeal for the Temple saturated His entire being.

The Temple was now controlled by the Jewish aristocracy and they were out to make a buck. His Father's House had become a den of thieves. This had become a normal setting during Passover week, and everyone had become numb to what shouldn't have been a part of Temple worship. Money changers and profiteers filled every square inch of the courts trying to exploit the poor and rich alike. Instead of worshippers on their knees seeking God, Jesus saw booths upon booths of traders trying to gouge every cent from the people who had come to the temple to offer their sacrifices.

For many of them their pilgrimage had been long. They couldn't afford to bring the required sacrifice from their homeland. The poor animal wouldn't have survived the trek. It was customary to buy the sacrificial lamb or dove outside the Temple enclosures. What Jesus saw as He entered was more than commerce and free trade. It was price gouging at its ultimate. It was exploitation of the poor. This was His Father's House and it had turned into a viper's nest. Righteous anger flooded His veins. The sight and smell of lust sickened Him. True worshippers were being denied access to worship because of love for the almighty coin.

His fervor and love for His Father's House ate Him up. He was consumed with jealousy for the honor of God's House and for the honor of His Father who is heaven. God's House was to be a house of prayer, and not a house of commerce, nor to be used for the pursuit of illegal profit. God's house was to be a sanctuary for all who sought the Lord in truth. It was the Lord's time to meet with His people so that they could reflect on the Lord's goodness.

What Jesus saw as He entered the Temple enclosure was a marketplace and sales shop. So with the ferocity of a jealous lover, He drove out the thieves and robbers. To those who sold the doves Jesus yelled, "Take these things out of here!" It was the exploitation of the poor and Jesus would have none of it.

Jesus is jealous for us. He wants us to come and worship Our Father who is in heaven. He wants us to leave all our business practices outside the temple and come bow down and give our all to prayer and worship. Zeal for His Father's house consumed Him then and consumes Him still.

The Viper's Nest

Avrahm stood in line with Leah and their two sons, Ephraim and Levi. They were weary. The road to Jerusalem was long and treacherous. Avrahm was a simple farmer of modest means, but he was also a faithful follower of Yahweh and committed to following the instructions of Moses.

He twirled the meager Roman coin over in the palm of his hand. It wasn't much. The harvest had been sparse this year. The spring rains were few and far between. Avrahm brought a tenth of his produce though. Somehow God will provide.

He and his family were true Israelites, and they had come to worship. They brought their offering of sacrifice. Their home was too far away to bring an animal sacrifice so he stood in line to purchase a dove, the offering of the poor. The Temple priests would not allow Roman coin to be used so Avrahm first had to exchange Roman coin for Temple coin.

As he approached the scales to weigh out his coin, Avrahm saw a Rabbi out of the corner of his eye. The Rabbi was weaving a braided whip with fury flowing into the strands. The Rabbi watched as the money changers weighed each pilgrim's coin. Avrahm knew it was a weighted scale. Everyone knew it. It was something they had grown accustomed to. It was an evil they had been desensitized from. What could an average farmer do about such injustices? It was simply a part of Temple life.

Just as Avrahm approached the money changer, the Rabbi flew through the Temple brandishing the newly braided whip. His name was Jesus and He was tossing the table before Avrahm. It was like observing a furious squall on the Sea of Galilee. Avrahm was at a loss, and just stood with mouth gaping as coins and gold flew everywhere. The lambs stampeded, bawling through the courts. Jesus chased the deceivers from the Temple with His whip of cords.

Avrahm's spirits soared as he witnessed this righteous display of anger in the House of God. Hadn't he wanted to do the exact same thing year after year? All he desired was to come and worship the Lord with his thanksgiving and sacrifice, but year after year these thieves had robbed him of worship. This man, this Rabbi, swarmed in and drove out all that defiled this temple.

Waypoints to your destination:

How did Jesus react to commercialism in His Father's house?

What have we compromised in worship that has led us away from a House of Prayer?

Have we exchanged convenience over sacrifice?

Have we allowed commercialism to set up camp in our Temple?

"Lord, I want to have Your zeal and fervor. Stir in me Your passion as I reflect on Your righteous indignation and jealousy over me. Make me into a House of Prayer."

Traveling to the Heart of Things

Day Twenty Four

"Now while He was in Jerusalem at the Passover Festival, many people saw the signs He was performing and believed in His name. But Jesus would not entrust Himself to them, for He knew all people. He did not need any testimony about mankind, for He knew what was in each person" John 2:23-24 NIV.

I kept watching him all service long. My son loved sitting in his papaw's lap during church. I was good with it because my dad could coral my three year old son and keep him from wandering the aisles during the preaching, but this particular service, my son just kept staring at his papaw's jugular. Pretty soon it went from just looking to touching, which went from just touching to flicking. I watched my son's mouth open from time to time as if he wanted to ask a question. I could hear my own mother's thoughts, "Oh son please don't say it. Please don't speak out loud for all to hear what you are dying to ask about." Before I could get out of my seat, my son audibly spoke what I knew was on his mind as he flicked the skin under my dad's chin. "Papaw, what's all that extra stuff hanging down?" I'm not sure anyone around could focus on the point of the sermon after that, I knew I couldn't. Have you ever been there? You are sitting with a child who just wants to

143

understand the world around them. Sometimes it is like you can see the questions forming on their lips, because you know your child so well.

This is what I think of as I read John 2:23-25. "When Jesus was in Jerusalem for the Passover Feast, many people believed in Him because they saw the miracles He did. But Jesus did not believe in them because He knew them all. He did not need anyone to tell Him about people, because He knew what was in people's minds" John 2:23-25 NCV.

I knew what was in my son's mind at this particular moment. I had been given certain signs that led to my precognitive knowledge of his next audible question, but when I focus on that last phrase in these verses, I stop short. What is in my mind? What are my thoughts that Jesus can read? I read Landry's mind that one and only time, but Jesus searches my thoughts and mind constantly. Jesus knows the level of my faith in him. What I speak and proclaim to others, Jesus knows the truth and the depth of my declarations. Jesus knows the true intent of each of my actions. Even more so than I truly understand. He perceives if they are from humility or for self-promotion.

This is hard for me to write. What am I doing? What is the hardline truth here? As I type away I am wondering, "Are these my own personal thoughts, or are these words flowing from God to me?" What is my true motivation here? I have been learning over the past year, as I write, that there is a truth Jesus is trying to instill in me. Jesus knows me better than I know myself. He knows my hidden agenda when at times I can't even see it.

That is where we find Him now. The Amplified Version in verse 23 says, "many believed in His name (identified themselves with His party) after seeing His signs (wonders, miracles) which He was doing."

Oh, how scripture transcends the ages. During the Republican and Democratic national conventions lines were drawn. Many were asking, "Which party do you identify with?" We may try to fool ourselves into thinking this is modern day, but Jesus walked through religious conventions every time He traveled thru Jerusalem. I don't have to wonder what He might think watching these national conventions unfurl; I can just read about it in John 2:23-25. "Jesus (for His part) did not trust Himself to them, because He knew all men." AMP version. "He Himself knew what was in human nature. (He could read men's hearts.)" NET version. "Many believed in Him because they saw His miracles. They wanted to see His "parlor tricks." Message Bible.

Luke 23:8 NIV says, "When Herod saw Jesus, he was greatly pleased, because for a long time he had been wanting to see Him. From what he had heard about Him, he hoped to see Him perform a sign of some sort."

Crowds were beginning to congregate around Jesus. He was just making his entrance into the public domain. Obviously, He was performing signs that no other person had exhibited before. The Bible doesn't say at this point what the miracles or wonders were, but whatever they were people wanted to see Him perform more. It is our nature. We are still doing it. We are intrigued by graphic you-tube videos. If there is a popular site with millions of hits, haven't you checked it out for yourself? We are also in a "show me" state of mind. "Jesus, show me what you can do for me and I will follow you."

We are no different than the people in Jerusalem were at this moment. Those in Jerusalem wanted His works; not His words. His words would be what led to conviction. Conviction, they could do without. Spectacular performance is what they came to see. That is what they clambered for, but Jesus desired sincerity from them. He desired friendship from them. He didn't want their praises because of the miraculous signs. He did not take pleasure in these. He desires repentant hearts that acknowledge the darkness inside them. He was the new kid on the block and they wanted Him to perform. This is what Jesus knew of man. He knew their true intent.

He looked out over all who came to follow Him. He knew each face already. He knew each heart. He saw the inner person because He was God, and He came from God. Jesus knew the wickedness of some before Him and He knew their weaknesses. They had come to hear the piper play, but the piper would not entrust Himself to them for He knew their true character.

Just as He knows my true character. He knew who would be a false friend and who would be His subtle enemy. He knew each pretentious face before Him. His knowledge did not come from anyone, not even Peter, or Andrew, or Philip, or Nathaniel. To them this was just a sea of unknowns. Jesus didn't need man's information. He is deity. His knowledge is infallible intuition born because He created each person who stood before Him that day.

Boy, were those words as harsh to read as they were to write? It was a hard scene for me to visit today. Like the boy in the movie, "Signs" with Mel Gibson, I want to wrap my head in aluminum foil to shield my thoughts from the One who knows me so well. But alas, that can never be. Just like I knew the words before they ever tumbled from Landry's lips, Jesus knows my every thought before it even crosses my mind. He knows my true inclination and the purity of my motives. As we have that precognitive intuition as to the next words that might flow from our child's mouth because we know them so well, Jesus knows us even deeper than that. He created each heart, and mind. His level of knowledge goes to the deepest recesses of our hearts.

God says in Genesis 8:21 NIV, "Every inclination of the human heart is evil from childhood..." So, where's my hope in all of this? Do I throw up my hands and give in to my natural instincts of evil? My hope is found in Psalm 51. I can pray each verse. "Purify me from my sin and I will be clean." "Wash me clean from my guilt." "Because of your great compassion." "Restore to me the joy of my salvation." "Renew a steadfast spirit within me."

I no longer have to try and hide my thoughts from God because the blood Jesus shed for me on the cross cleanses me from all my evil inclinations. He calls me to dwell on thoughts that are true, noble, right pure, admirable, excellent or praiseworthy. These are what I am to think on. He calls me to follow Him not because He can perform miracles, but because I love Him and believe in Him, and because I believe, then I will see the great and wonderful things He does for me.

The Discerner
The days had been long and draining. The energy He had spent cleansing His Father's house had consumed Him. Jesus could feel the animosity rising around Him. He had infuriated important people in the Temple as He threw out the vile scum and moneychangers. The number of influential enemies mounted against Him. He felt their angry stares even as His own voice crescendoed through the courts when He upended the tables of the traffickers while they marketed their sacrificial doves. Their accusations spewed from their lips. They demanded Him to prove His authority to do these things.

In the darkened halls of the Temple He caught the glimpse of His greatest foe. Jesus heard as Satan drug his nails across the white marble colonnades in the Temple. It was an annoying sound screeching across the air. He was the only One to hear it. He knew His age old enemy had come to stir up this havoc. Animosity and treachery were some of his most vile weapons. But no matter, zeal for His Father's House consumed Him. His passion lifted Him above all hatred.

Jesus had gotten His orders and His power from God. He knew what to do and when to do it. He could do nothing on His own; He could only do what His Father had given Him authority to do. So He went around Jerusalem ministering to the worshipful pilgrims who had thronged into Jerusalem this week to celebrate their deliverance from slavery in Egypt. The sick were healed, the lame had walked, and the deaf could hear.

Many believed in Him because of the miracles He performed this year in Jerusalem, but He knew their hearts. Jesus looked out at the sea of mankind gathered in this city. The loyal and the seeking had a glow about them. Jesus could see it in their eyes, as He looked deeper into their souls. Those who were in it for His showmanship and His spectacular signs had a come hither look about them. He knew they wouldn't last long. Then He looked at the Pharisees. That look was easily recognizable. Their disdain for Him was written across their faces.

He was the Discerner of all hearts. He had created each one. He knew what was in their minds and thoughts. And He would only entrust Himself to One, His Father who art in Heaven.

On the Way

Waypoints to your destination:

What was Jesus doing in Jerusalem after He cleansed the Temple?

Why did the people believe in Him?

Why do you think He did not entrust Himself to the people?

What do you think about as you realize the depth of knowledge Jesus has about you?

Does it make you want to guard your thoughts?

"Lord, You have searched me and You know me. You perceive my thoughts from afar. You know my going out and my lying down. Cleanse me O God. Blot out my transgressions and create in me a pure heart."

Visits in the Night

Day Twenty Five

"There was a man named Nicodemus who was one of the Pharisees and an important Jewish leader. One night Nicodemus came to Jesus and said, "Teacher, we know you are a teacher sent from God, because no one can do the miracles you do unless God is with him" John 3:1-2 NCV.

He came by night seeking the miracle worker. Nicodemus had been in the sea of people in Jerusalem that week. They had witnessed the signs and wonders Jesus had performed. Nicodemus saw Jesus drive out the temple merchants. He was a Pharisee. He was probably in the Temple compound. He would have had firsthand knowledge of Jesus' righteous indignation of His Father's House being treated so corruptly.

This new miracle worker must have intrigued Nicodemus. Jesus probably had the attention of every Pharisee in Jerusalem by this time. I don't know, maybe their little clique sent Nicodemus; maybe Nicodemus came on his own. The Bible doesn't say. All I know is Nicodemus came. Whatever Jesus had done or said that day in Jerusalem piqued the curiosity of this renown teacher of Israel. Even Jesus acknowledged Nicodemus with respect and with uniqueness.

"Jesus replied, 'Are you the teacher of Israel, and yet do not know or understand these things? (Are they strange to you?)" John 3:10 AMP. Three letters. T – H – E. (The) – it is an article in English grammar. Article words are used with nouns

150

to indicate the type of reference being made by the noun. Boring right? But as I read John 3:10 in the Amplified Version, I had to follow where my thoughts took me. "The" – an article that determines the noun. It is a qualifying word that denotes uniqueness. Jesus validated Nicodemus as THE teacher of Israel.

The teacher came by night to seek someone who performed things Nicodemus could never do. The teacher came by night to listen to a new teacher who taught with the wisdom of the ages. At times, I wish I could have been there in Jerusalem that day. I try to put myself on that side of history. What did Jesus do while in Jerusalem that caused this unique teacher of the law to seek out Jesus? Nicodemus said, "We know you are a teacher from God, because no one can do the miracles you do unless God is with him."

Again, what were those miracles? Whatever they were, the signs Jesus performed in the capital of Israel validated Jesus' God-given authority. You see, these Pharisees were a proud group. There were no newbies to their sect. A new teacher didn't just arrive on the scene. To be recognized by these guys, you had to have been trained and taught by the best of the best. Jesus was not recognized amongst Nicodemus' peers. No known Pharisee had ever trained Jesus. So where did this Galilean come from, and who gave Him his authority? Whatever signs and miracles Jesus had just exemplified had validated him in Nicodemus' eyes as a teacher sent from God.

Nicodemus was famous among those in Israel. He bore the title of "The teacher of Israel." He was renowned as a wise and learned man. People came to him seeking his wisdom, but for one night out of his life he laid down pride and prejudice and he came seeking someone with more than he possessed.

Jesus was a no one among Nicodemus' friends, but there was just something about this new preacher man. Whatever sly little glimpse he attained from Jesus on this day left him wanting more. So he slipped in quietly in the dark seeking Jesus' knowledge. He who had great knowledge sought Him with the greatest knowledge.

I humbly urge each of us: lay it down. Lay down all the wisdom that is in us and give diligent heed to seeking the One who contains the wisdom of the ages. Jesus came to this earth and wrapped inside of Him was the wisdom and knowledge that created the universe. He knows all things. He sees all our thoughts and He is the only one who has the solution for all our problems.

The Teacher of Israel

Nicodemus' thoughts were swirling. "Who was this Rabbi?" The dark of the night seeped into his thoughts. The myriad of stars hung like brilliant diamonds laid across black velvet. He hired one of the sparrow boys to lead him across the back alleyways of Jerusalem. The boy held his lamp high to light the way into the black night. A slight fog obscured the path before Nicodemus. He truly did not need his little guide tonight, but the little guy was enthralled in this mission, so he allowed the little sparrow to lead on.

Fivel held the hand of the teacher and led him. He was honored to light the way for this mighty teacher in Israel. They were off to see a new Rabbi. This clandestine mission was of utmost importance. His club foot kept him from a speedy journey. It always had. When the other sparrow boys got navigational jobs leading important Pharisees around Jerusalem, Fivel was most often overlooked because he was crippled, but Nicodemus searched him out. Fivel loved leading

The Teacher. Nicodemus had a deep baritone voice that soothed Fivel's fears. Nicodemus made Fivel forget his club foot. He focused on the path in front of him. This mission was important.

Jesus' voice had echoed through the Temple courts like a thousand voices bouncing off the marbled walls as He drove out the money changers and the merchants. His passion for Yahweh's House to become a House of Prayer and not a den of thieves, came in direct conflict with the elite of the religious leaders at the time.

Nicodemus observed their faces. Unabated savage hatred was written across each one. A cold knot wove within him. Fear for the Rabbi's life began to form in Nicodemus' mind. This fear was one of the reasons that motivated him to come seeking Jesus. Intrigue and curiosity drove him through the dark night. There was no denying it. Nicodemus was drawn to Jesus and he had to define this fascination.

Yeshua was a Rabbi like no other. Nicodemus held the highest office among his peers. He was The Teacher of Israel, but yet this Jesus did and performed signs that he could not do. No one he knew could speak and create and touch and heal like he had witnessed this Rabbi do.

All of Jerusalem was a buzz about these mighty acts of God. For that is what they were, acts of God. He must find out more. He looked at his little guide. Nicodemus had grown quite fond of little Fivel. Fivel, his name means light, and so he welded his torch to the heights of his length all the while dragging his useless leg across the dust of the path so he could light Nicodemus' way.

Fivel took great pride in leading this mission. "I wonder," Nicodemus thought to himself. "I wonder could this Rabbi named Jesus, could He possibly heal my little friend?" He let the thought remain unanswered this night.

Waypoints to your destination:

How does John 3:1 describe Nicodemus?

What do you think sent Nicodemus to Jesus?

How did he describe Jesus?

Read John 19:39. What do you think Nicodemus' final conclusion about Jesus was?

What can you learn from Nicodemus' actions?

"Lord, I come seeking you. I lay down all of my wisdom. I lay down all my knowledge and I come seeking the One who created it all. You alone are the Ancient of Days. You alone know the answers to all my questions."

The Meeting of the Minds

Day Twenty Six

"There was a man named Nicodemus who was one of the Pharisees and an important Jewish leader. One night Nicodemus came to Jesus and said, "Teacher we know you are a teacher sent from God, because no one can do the miracles you do unless God is with him" John 3:1-2 NCV.

Peace accords, Geneva Convention, the end of the Cold War, the signing of the Treaty of Versailles, and the list could go on and on. At some point nations seek out an end to war and debate and disagreements. Governmental heads of states join together in a meeting of minds to negotiate terms of surrender or to draw up articles of peace.

President Ronald Regan met with Mikhail Gorbachev at the Geneva summit. Both were seeking to cut nuclear weapons. Ulysses S Grant and General Robert E Lee met at Appomattox Court House in Virginia. Lee came to agree to Grant's term of surrender. This meeting brought an end to one of the bloodiest wars in American history.

Fascinating historical meetings have taken place throughout the centuries because polar opposite political factions come together either seeking peace and an end to bloodshed, or one comes to surrender insubjugation to another. Either way, they come to have a meeting of the minds. It is referred to as diplomacy. It is the art and practice of conducting negotiations between representatives of states.

There once was another diplomatic meeting that took place between two very famous teachers of Israel. Jesus and Nicodemus represented two opposite ends of the spectrum in their belief and knowledge about God.

Nicodemus was a Pharisee. He lived by the strictest possible religious rules. Nicodemus represented the best in the nation. He was a teacher, a Pharisee and a member of the Jewish ruling council, and yet he came seeking a meeting with "the teacher sent from God."

He came at night. Maybe he came to practice the art of diplomacy. Maybe he came to negotiate with Jesus and find a compromise to their different theological beliefs. Maybe those are the reasons he came, but what he got was the greatest salvation message known to man. John 3:16 has saved countless numbers of people from condemnation, myself included.

Jesus was and is the Son of God. Jesus was sent by God. He came to show grace and mercy and not legalism.

They were from polar ends of the spectrum. It was faith verses religion, and relationship verses legalism.

Nicodemus came on a sincere quest for truth. He had a deep religious hunger, but was blind to God's grace and mercy. Nicodemus sought out this Teacher who performed signs that no other teacher had the ability to perform. Nicodemus recognized a Teacher that was greater than himself, and because he came with his questions, we reap the benefits. Nicodemus came to Jesus and was present in the moment. He was all ears and full of questions. Because Nicodemus came with an open mind, we get instructed in the basics of salvation.

"For God so loved the world that He gave His one and only Son, that whoever believes in Him shall not perish but have eternal life" John 3:16 NIV.

"For God did not send his Son into the world to condemn the world, but that the world through Him might be saved" John 3:17 NKJV.

And because Jesus revealed true salvation to Nicodemus's sincere heart, as a little girl of eight years old, I believed in the declaration Jesus told Nicodemus. I secured my future in Jesus' kingdom.

"You will search for me. And when you search for me with all your heart, you will find me!" Jeremiah 29:13 NCV.

We live in a technological world. It is easier to email, text, inbox, message and Face Book than it is to take time out of our busy days to meet with friends and family face to face. Online sermons fill in when life takes you away from going to church. Trust me, I know. When you're gone for an entire summer, that's your option, but it still feels like something is missing.

Hebrews 10:24-25 in the NIV says, "And let us consider how we may spur one another on toward love and good deeds, not giving up meeting together, as some are in the habit of doing, but encouraging one another - and all the more as you see the Day approaching."

After being absent all summer, I walked into church one Sunday and received the actual fulfillment of this verse as my church family sincerely asked about me and my family. Technology is a dangerous way from excusing ourselves from social interaction.

For those of us who don't like confrontation and actually run away from it, it is hard to confront people. When we have a difference of opinions, it is sometimes uncomfortable to hash things out one on one. I fear we are a generation of people who are failing in diplomacy and it will soon become extinct. We hash out disputes over social media and emails instead of being present in the moment and trying to listen to each other and hear their heart.

Will face to face meetings become an archaic art? "Mano y mano." It literally means "hand and hand." We have placed this phrase in an adversarial context, but what if we really tried to walk hand in hand with those who differ from our opinions? What if we reached across the aisle and showed the world the great love of God? That's what Jesus did with Nicodemus, and because He did, I believe in God's salvation.

At the point of this meeting with Jesus, Nicodemus definitely had different opinions about obtaining God's favor than Jesus did. He believed his good works could buy God's blessing and he taught a nation on how to practice the Law of God. But for a night out of his life, he put those beliefs on the back burner. He came with an open mind and he was present in that moment. His thoughts didn't wander to how he could persuade Jesus to his own way of thinking.

Sometimes I wonder, do people really listen to one another? Do we really ever stop long enough to see one another's heart? I am one who is easily offended. Okay, I admit it. I am thin skinned. My feelings do get hurt by the slightest offense. I get upset if the waitress is rude, or if the sales clerk is abrasive. But do I ever walk away wondering what went wrong in their day that might have caused them to be cranky?

"So be careful how you listen. Those who have understanding will be given more. But those who do not have understanding, even what they think they have will be taken away from them" Luke 8:18 NCV.

Nicodemus did come by night, but thank God he came. He met with Jesus face to face. He asked his questions. Jesus shared with Nicodemus the heart of true salvation. Jesus revealed to Nicodemus the great and abiding love of God. " For God so loved the world that He gave His one and only Son..."

Nicodemus could have been ostracized by his peers because he acknowledged that Jesus was sent by God. The Bible doesn't say if Nicodemus walked away from that meeting a changed man, but in John 7:50-51 the Bible says he rebuked the Pharisees for condemning Jesus without hearing Him. The Pharisees were meeting to discuss what to do with this Jesus, but Nicodemus silenced their arguments by using their own laws.

"Nicodemus, who had gone to Jesus earlier and who was one of their own number, asked, "Does our law condemn a man without first hearing him to find out what he has been doing?" John 7:51 NCV.

And even later, Nicodemus helped Joseph of Arimathea bury Jesus.

"Later, Joseph of Arimathea asked Pilate for the body of Jesus. Now Joseph was a disciple of Jesus, but secretly because he feared the Jewish leader. With Pilate's permission, he came and took the body away. He was accompanied by Nicodemus, the man who earlier had visited Jesus at night. Nicodemus brought a mixture of myrrh and aloes, about seventy-five pounds" John 19:38-39 NCV.

I believe Nicodemus was changed through this meeting of the minds. He was changed for the better because of his exchange with Jesus. We can be changed also because of this meeting between these two teachers. The words spoken by Jesus to Nicodemus led me to believe in the Son of God. I believe that God so loved me. I believe that God gave His one and only Son to die in my place. I believe because of Jesus' death, burial, and resurrection, I will have everlasting life. I believe I will live with Jesus forever in heaven in a home that He is preparing for me.

I encourage each of us to be a Nicodemus. Go to Jesus. Have a meeting of the minds. Go with an honest, open heart, and be present in the moment. Don't try to convince Jesus of all the ways He can help you. Jesus already knows your need. Just lay aside your agenda and take up His agenda for the meeting. Then let Jesus tell you of God's great love for you.

His Agenda

Jesus met with His Father. The morning was cool and the air was brisk. The vapor from His lungs left a small fog as He breathed in and out. Springtime in Jerusalem clung to the last elements of winter's morning. It was still early. Dawn had not yet broken on the horizon, but Jesus loved this time of day. It was His and His alone. No one had yet intruded into these moments. His friends were still sleeping in the guesthouse. He had closed the door on their muffled snoring.

The stars above were bidding Him come to meet with their Creator. Jesus knew each one by name and why He had helped hang them in their proper constellation. The heavens above Him declared the handiwork of His Father. Slipping out the Shushan gate, He pled for mercy upon those who dwelt in this city. Their ignorance begged for grace and mercy as Jesus climbed up the Mount of Olives.

The aroma of olives filled His nostrils with their fragrance. His knees pressed oil out of fallen olives when He bowed in homage to His Father who was in Heaven. These quiet moments with His Fathers mapped out what His day would hold.

Every moment was filled with abundance. His creation needed His mercy and His power. The signs and wonders were pouring from Him now. Here in this City of David, Jesus had healed and restored many. His compassion for them flowed from the seat of his emotions. His gut reactions were to reach out and give them all that God had planned for Him, but He could only do what His Father in Heaven instructed Him to do. So He restrained only because He came to do the LORD's bidding.

"Our Father who art in Heaven," Jesus began and the Father responded. "You will receive a visitor in the late nighttime hours," God informed His Son. "His name is Nicodemus. He will come seeking answers and ask You, "Who has given you this authority?" Nicodemus is set in his ways. His thoughts are not our thoughts, but this conversation You will have with Him is of utmost importance and it will transcend through the ages. Make sure John is present. He will record this meeting, and for all generations to come many will believe in me because of the words you will declare to Nicodemus. Here is Your agenda for the meeting of the minds. Tell him that because of My great love for all the world, I have sent You into the world. I have sent You from My realm to tell the world and to show the world what I am like."

The Father gave His Son the full specifics of the meeting. Jesus listened carefully. He would repeat every word for He lived and existed on this earth to please the One He was talking to right now.

Kellye Jones

Waypoints on the way to your destination:

Why do you think Nicodemus came to Jesus?

When did Nicodemus come to Jesus?

What were some of the questions on his mind?

What does Nicodemus' example provide for us?

"Lord, I come to You. You are my meeting place, and only You have the perfect timeline for my days ahead. At times I come in the darkest part of my nights to seek You because You alone have all my answers."

Jerusalem in the Rear View Mirror

Day Twenty Seven

"Then Jesus and His disciples left Jerusalem and went into the Judean countryside. Jesus spent some time with them there, baptizing people" John 3:22 NLT.

We had just dropped Mom off at her house on Mingo. The heat was stifling. The temperature was 100 with a heat index of 109. I was over it and done with these oven baking temperatures. We were driving past the heavy brush that encompasses Mingo street. The recent rains lay puddled and stagnant in the ditches. I cringed because I knew in the midst of all this green lavish foliage lay mosquitos and ticks that could cart off a small rat.

Kevin asked, "How would you have like to have been a Sooner and blaze through all those trees in this heat?" My simple reply, "Honey, if you came to me one day and told me that was in your heart, I would just have to say, 'See ya next year." Seriously, I am just not a trailblazer and I don't do heat and bugs.

What does that say about me? What would I have done 2000 years ago if Jesus had asked me to follow Him then? Following Jesus seems exhausting to me. He and His disciples had to be in good physical health to travel the terrain as they did.

Kevin and I sometimes drive 14 hours in a car to travel to Pittsburgh. We try to psych each other up as we face the trip, each dreading the cramped car seats. I play the seat adjustment buttons like they are a piano keyboard. The heated and air cooling seats are switched on and off like a light switch. It's a long trip, but observing Jesus' traveling band, I'm thankful I have a car to travel in. They traipsed through Israel on two feet. Jesus traveled a great deal during the three years of His public ministry. Always coming and going. He had a mountain of work ahead of Him. He did become weary, but there were many souls to save. So, He traveled.

Jesus was ever faithful to follow the commands of God. He most certainly would have traveled to Jerusalem multiple times throughout the year to obey and celebrate the festivals as written in Leviticus. Though He traveled to Jerusalem often, He didn't tarry there long. As soon as His business was conducted, Jesus and His entourage would be off.

This time He led His little band north into Judea. His preaching and miracles had made a lot of noise in Jerusalem, now it was time for privacy. Jerusalem was the fountain head of the current gossip and the news media. If anything was note-worthy, you heard it in Jerusalem first.

So, Jesus exited this fine city. He withdrew into quieter settings, the hills of Judea. Those that flocked to Him in Jerusalem would not follow Him into the quieter countryside of Judea. He went on with His disciples, and there He paused. The traveling shoes were placed by the back door for a time.

"Jesus spent some time with them there, baptizing people" John 3:22b.

In the Greek, the words, "spent some time" is the word "diatribos." It means to thoroughly and successfully form a path by constant rubbing. This constant rubbing becomes a route and a regular path that leads someplace. Have you ever tried to grow grass in the paths your dog takes on a daily basis to the back fence? It's an almost impossible task.

Jesus spent some time with his disciples and with the people of Judea. There He would cut out a route that would lead many to believe in Him.

It is called the "road of faith." It is a worn and beaten road. This time spent in the Judean hillside became a spiritual journey the people took so that they could know God for who He truly was. He was the bridegroom inviting the people to dance to the pulse of His Father's heartbeat.

Like a trailblazer who took a machete to slice a trail through jungle brush, Jesus cut a path through the unsettled crowd of Jerusalem into the quiet territory of Judea and there He stayed awhile with the people. The traveling sandals came off. He took a break here so He could develop a group of people who would know the heart of God.

It was still the first year of Jesus' public ministry. It had not been that long since He Himself had come out of these very same baptismal rivers. He had been on the go since that moment, but now He hit the pause button. Jesus stayed with the people awhile here at the Jordan River so He could offer them a baptism of repentance.

His cousin, John the Baptist, was just up the river doing the same type of work. Remnants of Israel followed the path Jesus had blazed. They went down to the river to pray and to know The God of Israel.

John the writer gave us our timeline. Verse 24 of the NIV, "(This was before John was put in prison.)" Time was short. Relationships had to be nurtured so Jesus paused so He could reveal His Father's love to a group of people starving for a movement of their great God.

Jesus was our pioneer blazing trails to a personal relationship with our Heavenly Father. Like the Sooners of Oklahoma, His schooner cut ruts through brushy territory. The path He blazed is our road of faith. It is a highway leading to the kingdom of our God. Have you taken it yet?

All the way our Shepherd leads holding our hands. He hacks His way across the jungle that blocks our pathway to God. The obstacles blocking us are as vapor to Him.

Each of us have a great need to be led through life by Jesus. Our faith is the footprints we leave as we follow His rutted out path. Our steps may shuffle with weariness, but at the end of this road we will find a river flowing with abundant energy and life.

Down to the River to Pray

Ava looked dejectedly at her feet as she faltered along the path. The scorn of Rabbi Yosef's rebuke still left a crimson stain across her cheeks. She had offered what she could at the Temple this Passover. Her poor widow's mite clanged a lonely gong as she dropped it onto the currency scales.

Yacob had been laid to rest two years hence. She and her young son, Eli, were living off their last bit of savings. Ava felt the stares of pity all the way to her soul. Abundant life had been robbed from her and her son that dark day when she buried her loving husband, Yacob.

Married at age 16, Ava had no skills. Yacob had been a good provider earning a modest income. They had great plans until the day Ava noticed the white infection in Yacob's fingertips. They had gone to Rabbi Yosef and heard the dreaded cry, "Unclean, unclean! This man is a leper."

On the Way

Ava still felt the sting of tears as they rolled down her cheeks the day Yacob packed up and left for the colony. On that day her heart grew as numb as the limbs and appendages of Yacob's hand. The disease took a few short months before it claimed another life of a beloved husband and father.

Her soul was void, and her demeanor was humiliated as family and friends alike scorned and avoided Ava and her son. She traveled down this blazed path empty and without energy.

A new Rabbi had been teaching down by the river. The reports that reached her ears brought a wind of hope with them. She had actually witnessed Jesus turn over the scales of the money changers. She watched when her widow's mite flew into the air along with the myriad of other coins weighed out that day.

As her feet shuffled along this path, she felt as each footprint embedded into the trodden path matched her own. The gait and the rhythm matched her stumbling steps. Then she heard His voice. The sound of it touched her soul and she felt a rush of adrenaline pulse through her heart. When she reached the source of the voice thundering from the edge of the river, Ava paused. The look in this Rabbi's eyes were filled with love. Yeshua looked straight at her. For the first time in over a year Ava did not feel ostracized. She felt accepted and esteemed, all because Jesus looked at her with a depth of love that flowed from Heaven above.

Deliberately, intentionally she walked down to the river's edge. She desperately needed Jesus. It was a wrinkle in time, but at that moment her soul thirsted for the life Jesus offered. She pressed her hand into the hand of one of His friends. Simon grasped it firmly and led her down into the waters of the Jordan River.

Kellye Jones

Waypoints to you destination:

What does John 3:22 say that Jesus did?

What does this say to you about our Lord?

What path has Jesus blazed for you to travel?

Where do you think this path will lead?

"Lord, keep me on the highway to heaven. This road of faith is hard but it is also life giving. Jesus I press into you. Give me courage to continue on through these hardened roads that lead me to You."

God's Route

Day Twenty Eight

"Jesus knew the Pharisees had heard that He was baptizing and making more disciples than John (though Jesus Himself didn't baptize them – His disciples did. So he left Judea and returned to Galilee. He had to go through Samaria on the way" John 4:1-4 NLT.

My GPS comes to life the moment I switch the engine on. I plug in my address and plot my route. Which route do you choose as you plot your way on your navigational system? I always choose the fastest route. At times the shortest route takes you through stop light after stop light, and here in Tulsa it may even lead you to take a detour or two. The fastest route usually leads to turnpikes and main highways which have no stop lights.

Jesus' navigational guide was different. He was not given a choice between fastest, shortest, least traveled, or less dangerous. His route was always God's route.

There were three routes to take from Judea to Galilee. To the Jewish person of Jesus' day Samaria was a disgusting country with a questionable history. So, the route many a Jew took was to cross east over the Jordan River and head north. This route avoided traveling through the country of Samaria. A second route would take a pious Jew west up the coastline of the Mediterranean Sea, also allowing the avoidance of getting their sandals dirty from Samaritan soil.

The third route was to head straight north through the country of Samaria. On this day that was the route Jesus chose.

"Now He had to go through Samaria" John 4:4 NIV.

"He had..." Had is the verb for this version. He was on a divinely appointed schedule and He had a divinely appointed route to take. His Heavenly Father had a schedule that Jesus must keep. A certain well in Samaria was the meeting place.

The Samaritans were a mixed breed, part Jew and part gentile. Their history grew out of the Assyrian captivity of Northern Israel in 727 B.C. Once settling back in the land, the Samaritans could not prove their genealogy and so were rejected by the puritans of the Jewish race. They were barred from Temple worship, so they established their own Temple and religious practices on Mount Gerizim. The fires of prejudice raged intensely. No true Jew would set foot in the land of Samaria.

Jesus was different. He was a reformist, His teachings were radical, and He ignited a social movement that spread like a wild fire across the Roman Empire. He did not conform to the outrageous religious practices of the Jewish hierarchy nor did He keep to the prevailing social customs of the day, and because He did not, His enemies were always hot on His trail. This was the position He found Himself in while He was teaching and His disciples were baptizing in Judea. The Pharisees were trying to incite competition between Jesus and John the Baptist. This was not His time to be arrested so Jesus and His disciples headed north. It was the fastest route, but it was also the way His Heavenly Father revealed to Him.

"So He came to a town in Samaria called Sychar, near the plot of ground Jacob had given to his son Joseph. Jacob's well was there, and Jesus, tired as He was from the journey, sat down by the well. It was about noon" John 4:5-6 NIV.

They had walked the equivalent of a marathon. There were hills and valleys that dotted the terrain. It was Israel and it was hot. Jesus entered our world completely God and completely human. He had all our weaknesses and was subject to all our physical labors. So yeah, Jesus sat down by the well tired. Deep fatigue had settled over Him. He was on the run from His enemies; He was trying to lead and teach a rag tag group of disciples; and to top it off, He had just walked almost 26 miles. There were no restaurants along the way. No Love's Rest Stops to grab a snack. He was fixed on this route laid out before Him and He stayed the course. Why? There was a certain woman who needed to be shown His grace.

The twists and turns of this journey had led Him this far, so He sat to wait for His next appointment. They were all hungry and tired. He sent His disciples into town to get some food. Jesus was alone as was the woman who came to draw water from Jacob's well. She sized Him up all the while He knew everything about her.

In these moments with the woman at the well Jesus broke every protocol known to Jewish man at the time. He spoke to her.

"When a Samaritan woman came to the well to get some water, Jesus said to her, 'Please give me a drink.'" John 4:7 NCV.

A Jewish Rabbi speaking to a woman; a Jewish Rabbi speaking to a Samaritan; and then a Jewish Rabbi speaking to a Samaritan woman of obvious ill-repute, well, that was three strikes against the social norm. His question surprised her.

"The woman said, 'I am surprised that you ask me for a drink, since You are a Jewish man and I am a Samaritan woman.' (Jewish people are not friends with Samaritans.) John 4:9 NCV.

In the Jewish belief system the water she would draw from the well would have been polluted because it had been handled by a woman, a Samaritan, and a woman living a scandalous life. It would have been sacrilege to drink from her vessel, and Jesus would have been considered ceremonially unclean. It was unheard of for a Rabbi to even speak to a woman in public, but Jesus threw all religion out the window. To Him she was a woman in need and only He could fill her need.

At first she tried to detour Him around her real need. She wanted to talk about religious practices and the different worship places of Samaritans verses the Jewish people. She wanted Him to go around her sin, but Jesus would not be derailed.

"Jesus told her, 'Go get your husband and come back here.' The woman answered, "I have no husband." Jesus said to her, 'You are right to say you have no husband. Really you have had five husbands, and the man you live with now is not your husband. You told the truth'" John 4:16-18 NCV.

Jesus met her at the point of her greatest need. He came into her messy life. She and her jar were empty but Jesus filled it with living water. We were never given her name, but her story was written so that all generations could know how far Jesus will travel to rescue us from ourselves.

Jesus is still doing this today. He puts aside our beliefs, our culture, and our prejudices, and He meets us in our everyday activities and quenches our every thirst. As the childhood worship song goes, "Red and yellow, black and white, they are precious in His sight. Jesus loves the little children of the world."

There is nothing too empty or void that He cannot fill. There is no sin too dark that He cannot cast His light upon it. No thought so hidden that He does not know, and there is no dirt that He cannot clean. There is no boundary He will not cross to come to our rescue. All He asks of us is to make the trip to the well.

The Walk of Shame

Rahab listened as the door closed on her misery. She felt so dirty and soiled. He used her. She knew this. He escaped every night from his nag of a wife, but every morning he would slither back to their home and away from Rahab.

How could she blame him? She allowed this type of behavior. She had been here before. No man had seemed permanent in her life. Not even her own father. She wasn't even sure if she desired permanence from them. Every relationship stole a part of her worth. Slowly ever so slowly, her soul was eroding from inside of her. Rahab was lost in a sea of shame and disgrace.

The sun was finally overhead and morning had passed. All reputable women of the village were safe under their roofs kneading bread and steadying their homes for their men and children. It was her time to step into the world. She had been separated from all the good in the village. She was a woman of the night. All social events for her began in the shroud of darkness. Her moments in the sun happened in the loneliness of her walk.

Rahab had no other woman to accompany her to Jacob's well. Every morning as she heard the incessant bantering and gossiping of the women of the village, Rahab would close her shutters to their chatter. There had been many a time she heard her name mentioned. Though she tried to choke out the flood of

173

tears, they still escaped streaking down her cheeks. She was not immune to the stab of pain their words would strike.

Rahab carried her empty jug down to the well. The heat rose as vapor along her path. Her skin was tanned because of this routine, but it was her only option available to her.

Her hand rose to shield her eyes against the sun's rays. That's when she saw Him. He was a Jewish Rabbi. She was certain. He looked so tired. When she approached the well He startled her. He asked for a drink.

Rahab spoke her mind. She had never learned the art of keeping quiet, and this Rabbi welcomed her company. It was as if He knew their paths would intersect.

She came to the well empty. Shame and disgrace had stolen her soul, but this Man filled her emptiness. Disgrace was replaced with grace.

Rahab left her empty water jug and ran back to the village filled because Living Water had been poured into her. She would return to retrieve the dry container. Her thirst was quenched for the moment but she wanted more. This jug would be her reason for returning. She knew Jesus would fill it with more life-giving water.

On the Way

Waypoints to your destination:

What did you learn about Jesus from this encounter?

What do you think of the relationship Jesus initiated with the woman at the well?

How can you apply her story to your life?

Describe a time when Jesus sought you out and removed your sin and replaced it with His grace.

"Lord, thank You for crossing every dividing line. Thank you for coming into my messy world. Thank You for Your grace that removes my disgrace."

Sychar

Day Twenty Nine

"Many of the Samaritans in that town believed in Jesus because of what the woman said: "He told me everything I ever did." When the Samaritans came to Jesus, they begged Him to stay with them, so He stayed there two more days. And many more believed because of the things He said. They said to the woman, "First we believed in Jesus because of your speech, but now we believe because we heard Him ourselves. We know that this man really is the Savior of the world" John 4:39-42 NCV.

The name of their village means, "the end," but on this day it was their beginning. They came out of their homes to listen to her words, and then followed her, crossing the village limits to see this Man she was talking about. Her words stimulated their curiosity and were the beginning point of their belief system, but when Jesus spoke, it was His words that drove them to full-fledged belief. "We believe because we heard Him ourselves."

Her testimony wasn't eloquent. In fact it even had a questioning tone to it. "Come and see a man who told me everything I ever did! Could He possibly be the Messiah?" John 4:29 NLT. If you want to convince someone in a debate, you can't waver in your convictions. Here she stood not five minutes removed from the Rabbi who knew all about her, yet she ends her testimony questioning who He might be. This was where the power of God kicked in. He doesn't need us to speak with the tongue of men and angels. God just needs us to speak. Open our mouths and tell our testimony. It is God who will spark the flame of curiosity in others.

"They triumphed over him by the blood of the Lamb and by the word of their testimony;" Revelation 12:11a NIV.

Her communion with Jesus caused ripples in the life of a village. The moments Jesus spent with her left an indelible mark across her countenance and it caused others to sit up and take notice. The woman and her Savior had a tangible interaction that brightened her day, and she in turn brought Son light into the village of Sychar.

It was a win, win type of day. A woman of ill repute found her worth because the Son of God met with her at a lonely well. The people of Sychar found their worth because the Savior of the world crossed gridlines, man-made boundaries of human prejudices, and protest marches just so He could reveal His Father's love. He showed His disciples that there is worth in every man, woman, and child no matter what their skin color was, or what the state of their religious ideological stance was.

That is who Jesus was and who He still is today. He took the time out of an exhausting day to meet with people and give them value. "When they came out to see Him, they begged Him to stay in their village. So He stayed for two more days, long enough for many more to hear His message and believe" John 4:40-41 NIV. It did not matter to Him that they were Samaritans and despised by His fellow countrymen. When they begged Him to stay longer, He did. Jesus had a message to deliver and He spoke His words to people who wanted to hear it.

Jesus had left Judea just a few days back. He was traveling to a destination. He wanted to return to Galilee. He had been in Jerusalem, camped in the hills of Judea, and now He was on a layover on the way to Galilee. This layover was in the land of Samaria. Instead of allowing this layover to become an annoyance to Him, He spent His energy pouring out His Father's love and crossing racial prejudices. Jesus extended His layover because of their sincere desire to fellowship with Him.

"But you will receive power when the Holy Spirit comes on you; and you will be my witnesses in Jerusalem, and in all Judea and Samaria, and to the ends of the earth" Acts 1:8 NIV.

Jesus was modeling for the disciples what they would one day do. These very men who were traveling with Jesus through Samaria at this time would be instructed to tell the whole world all that they witnessed as they walked side by side with Him.

As with all great teachers, Jesus gave them a tangible example of how they were to do it and it began here on this leg of their journey. All it took was the sacrifice of time. The power of the Holy Spirit was already upon Him, in Him, and surrounding Him. The words and the will to speak of His Father's love and to engage in the lives of the neglected were birthed in the place of His great compassion and brokenness for these people.

In the confinement of man-made boundaries and human prejudices, and may I dare say, raciest ideology, Jesus broke all societal practices. His example of inclusionary love broke the gridlines of protest marches. Jesus was history's most radical leader. Jesus was the cutting edge of sacrificial love. His was a love the world needs now.

A whole village came to be included in the love of God because one woman was changed when she met His Son. Jesus impacted her life because He didn't judge or condemn. He gave her worth and value. Those two assets caused her to lift up her head and speak to people who had once degraded her. What Jesus instilled in her during that exchange at Jacob's Well gave her the courage to speak, and because she spoke, a village was inspired. When they sought Him, they found Him. When they invited, He stayed.

Jesus began this leg with a destination in mind, but on the way He took the time to love and engage in people's lives.

As I write, I look at the neighborhood I live in. What would happen if I opened my mouth and spoke my testimony?

The Well of Wrestling

Aheb was addicted to her forbidden scent. Night after night he entered her home cloaked in a black hooded robe. Every morning he would creak open Rahab's back door and sneak out before the sun's rays could reveal his identity to his neighbors. He couldn't risk being exposed. Aheb had married well. His wife's dowry was the down payment for his market. He traded in silk and perfume.

It was how he met Rahab. She came to his shop in the heat of the day when the wives of the town had finished their trading. Rahab was always in the market for the alluring and exotic scents from the east.

The townspeople knew him as honest and trustworthy. Aheb bartered back and forth with friends and neighbors all the while his dark secret marred his conscience.

He saw Rahab walking to the well alone eyes downcast. He knew she avoided the stares of those who judged her. With his heart guarded Aheb joined the rest who ostracized Rahab. He knew he shouldn't, but he couldn't help himself; he felt sympathy for her. He knew he was a culprit to her loneliness, but he reasoned she'd had many lover's before him. Her life was not his to worry about.

Aheb averted his eyes as she looked into the market square. Rahab was searching for acceptance among those out and about that day, but he could not cave. He dared not or his lies would be exposed also.

He wrestled all afternoon with a guilt that plagued him when he saw her running up the path from the well. She met his gaze full on. She was different from the moments he saw her leaving. Rahab entered the village head held high as if she were a queen. Her eyes gleamed and shone with assurance.

Aheb listened to her words and had followed other villagers to Jacob's well. He too met the traveling Rabbi. When Jesus looked at him straight on, Aheb could tell this Man knew all his secrets, but His look was not one of condemnation or judgement. Jesus' look encompassed him, giving him a desire to change. He listened to Jesus' words as Jesus stood between the mountains of blessing and cursing, preaching to a village called, "End." Sychar and its villagers would begin again on a new day with promises of blessing spoken by the Savior of the world.

Aheb approached Jesus with head downcast in shame. He wrestled with emotions of holding onto his secret life or embracing a new life of peace and freedom from his guilt.

Rahab was different. He could tell her lifestyle would be different from that point forward. Jesus had changed her for the better. There would be no more late night visits to her bedchamber for any man. Aheb was happy for her. He didn't know why. Something was happening in him. In his heart his addiction for her was melting away like lava down a volcano.

On the Way

Jesus' words were a catalyst shaping and transforming his thoughts and needs. Aheb would return to his wife with a full loving heart. He looked into the darkness of the well. In that moment Aheb stopped wrestling and took the hand of this traveling Rabbi.

Waypoints to your destination:

What was the reason the Samaritans first started believing?

What happened when they had firsthand communion with Jesus?

What had Jesus done for her?

Do you ever feel like you just aren't good enough to testify about Jesus?

How can God become bigger than your feelings of worthlessness?

"Lord, thank You for crossing the boundaries of time and space and prejudice. Thank You. Because of You I am worthy. Because of Your story I have a story to share."

The Return Trip

Day Thirty

"When Jesus heard that John had been arrested, He left Judea and returned to Galilee. He went first to Nazareth" Matthew 4:12-13a NLT.

"At the end of the two days, Jesus went on to Galilee. He Himself had said that a prophet is not honored in His own hometown. Yet the Galileans welcomed Him, for they had been in Jerusalem at the Passover celebration and had seen everything He did there" John 4:43-45 NLT.

"Then Jesus returned to Galilee, filled with the Holy Spirit's power. Reports about Him spread quickly through the whole region" Luke 4:14 NLT.

The computer screen glares at me like a coiled rattlesnake ready to strike. I walk away and look out the window biting my bottom lip in consternation. I drum my fingers across the wall. "Where to start? Where do these verses lead me? What rabbit hole will I tumble down today?" I turn back to the computer screen. This time the glow seems like a lighthouse on the cliffs of Dover beckoning me to follow the light past the breakers.

I hear the call of God trying to navigate me into safe harbor. I approach the keyboard with fear and trepidation not wanting to expose my frailties and weaknesses through the pages of this book. I don't want the cracks in my faith foundation exposed for all to read.

I am full of "what ifs." "What if the words don't come? What if this chapter isn't powerful enough?" Then come the, "Who are you's?" "Who are you to write devotionals? Who are you to write about the majestic King of Kings? Who are you to give lessons in faith?" The "what ifs" and the "who are you's" scream at me like a banshee in the night stealing my courage to write. "No one will read what you have to say, especially people in your hometown. Your family has witnessed many of your breakdowns. Are you supposed to write for them? Where is your PHD in biblical studies?" I cover my ears and squeeze my eyes shut. "Fix your thoughts on things of Heaven," I chant to myself.

Don't get me wrong I love writing and researching, but most of all I love the lessons the Lord teaches me, and the truths I must uncover. Each day is like a treasure hunt, digging to find the priceless pearl buried in the pages of Scripture waiting for me to unearth it. I fall to my knees, "God speak to me. Take my fingers and fill them with the words of men and angels. Don't let me be a clanging gong or a broken cymbal." He speaks, "Am I enough? Have I failed you yet? Are not these lessons exactly what you need for this day? Do you not see the relevance they are to your world? I AM all you need."

I invite the Author of the Book to come and sit in the rocking chair on my front porch. With heart open I bow at His feet as He rocks and pulls out the Age Old Book with tattered bindings. Life-giving water pours out of His mouth into my thirsty soul. I put away my fear that I'm just not good enough. His words encourage me and give me the lesson I need for such a time as this.

Jesus gave out of His brokenness and weakness. He came to the village of Sychar tired and thirsty, yet He gave them Living Water. He stayed with these lovely people for two days.

"When they came out to see Him, they begged Him to stay in their village. So He stayed for two days, long enough for many more to hear His message and believe" John 4:40-41 NLT.

Jesus took time out of His busy schedule to stay in a country that had been ostracized by His own country-men. They invited Him in and He went, eating their food, enjoying their fellowship, and teaching them truths from His Father. No other Rabbi in Jerusalem or Israel thought these people worthy to receive nuggets of wisdom from God Almighty. Jesus even spoke His first "I AM" statement to a woman whom the world had discarded. "I AM the Messiah!" John 4:26 NLT. She was the first to receive this clear declaration of truth to whom He admitted to be. Jesus loved people and He was enjoying this adventure on the way to the cross. I get ready to pack for my trip to Ethiopia learning from His example.

Then He receives word from Judea. His cousin John, the very one who'd immersed Him into the baptismal waters, was taken prisoner. Jesus and John shared a bond. Both had seen the heavens opened. Both had heard, "This is my beloved Son with whom I am well pleased." It was a moment that knit them together heart and soul, but now one of the two had been imprisoned. Jesus felt this deeply. He knew it was done because of a corrupt government and religious system, but He couldn't stop. He had places to go and souls to save. It wasn't His time yet, and He must stay one step ahead of those who would choose to take Him prisoner also. Jesus headed north into Galilee.

His heart had to have been breaking because of His friend and cousin, but in His brokenness He comes back into the land of Galilee empowered by the Holy Spirit of God. Crowds gathered as word of His return spread. Many in the crowd had seen what He had done in Jerusalem that year at the Passover celebration. Jesus was a rock star and the masses went out to see Him, and He went to them. It became His custom each Sabbath to go into their synagogues and read scripture.

"When He came to the village of Nazareth, His boyhood home, He went as usual to the synagogue on the Sabbath and stood up to read the Scriptures. The scroll of Isaiah the prophet was handed to Him" Luke 4:16-17a NLT.

He was the hometown hero that had been going around the countryside performing magical signs of healing that no other Rabbi could do. Of course Jesus would have been the one chosen to do the reading on this Sabbath day.

I love that even in His travels, Jesus did not neglect worship. The meeting together with His brothers and sisters was important to Him. He was not so fixated on His to do list and His places to be, that He forgot to keep the Sabbath Holy.

It was customary at this time that synagogue worship leaders invited a worthy person in the congregation to read from the Scriptures and comment on the reading. Jesus was definitely a noteworthy visitor to their congregation. Here was a Man who had grown up in their town. These people knew Him and they knew His parents, and here He was with an entourage and a following.

"He unrolled the scroll and found the place where this was written:

'The Spirit of the Lord is upon me, for He has anointed me to bring Good News to the poor. He has sent me to proclaim that captives will be released, that the blind will see, that the oppressed will be set free, and that the time of the Lord's favor has come.' He rolled up the scroll, handed it back to the attendant, and sat down. All eyes in the synagogue looked at Him intently" Luke 4:17-20 NLT.

These are the first verses in the chapter of Isaiah 61 plus or minus a few. The phrase, "He has sent me to comfort the brokenhearted" was omitted. Jesus did not describe, "The day of God's anger against their enemies," from verse 2. On this day in that synagogue Jesus chose not to focus on driving out the despised Roman legion from the land of the Galileans.

There was a more pressing need before Him. Broken, oppressed people were among those in attendance. The people were living in darkness and they were captives of the night. This was their greatest need and that was the brokenness He chose to focus on.

"Then He began to speak to them. 'The Scripture you've just heard has been fulfilled this very day!'" Luke 4:21 NLT.

He continued in His explanation of this passage. This was the customary order of service in the Synagogues on Sabbath, but His explanation inflamed them. This hometown Boy insulted their lineage. He didn't speak the words that they wanted to hear. Instead Jesus spoke the truth. These Galilean Jews needed to be saved by grace in the same manner as the Gentile pagans.

Jesus struck a blow to their Jewish pride. In the matter of minutes it took for His reading and His explanation, the people of His hometown went from admiration to fury. His words in verses 23 – 27 stirred their wrath. A whole Synagogue of people jumped up and mobbed Him. The energy of their anger forced Him to the side of the cliffs that their village was built on, but Jesus being filled with the dynamite power of the Holy Spirit, slipped through their hands like a knife through melted butter. He simply walked away.

We talk today of the divided political climate of our nation. Some think the winds of antagonism have polarized this country in ways never before witnessed. I say, "These are the gales and storms Jesus faced every step He took on the way to the cross."

Jesus knew full well what He was walking into that day He arrived in Nazareth. "A prophet is not honored in his hometown." Yet, He went to His hometown and taught as He was in the habit of doing. That took courage which comes from the power of the Holy Spirit bottled inside of Him.

I tap into that same power now so that I may write. My fingers tap along the keyboard forming the words of courageous lessons taught to me by a powerful Savior.

The Hometown Boy

Phineas, the worship leader of the Synagogue of Nazareth, stood in the front of the processional to welcome this hometown Teacher. He couldn't wait to see the tricks this Magician had up His sleeve. Phineas had recently returned to Nazareth along with his fellow tribesmen from their pilgrimage south to Jerusalem to celebrate the Passover.

He had seen this young Rabbi perform many unexplainable signs in Jerusalem this year. The whole city buzzed with the latest chatter about Jesus of Nazareth, and here He was walking into their village. Phineas was the first to greet Jesus. He grasped Jesus' hand tightly and brought Him in for the customary greeting, a kiss on each cheek three times.

Great expectation filled everyone in Nazareth. Pride swelled in them for they felt they had a hand in raising this fine young Rabbi. Maybe Jesus would make mention of their goodness to Him as a child.

As they welcomed Jesus into their community, each chin was raised a little higher because of the part they'd played in His childhood. It simply left their thoughts of the days they had whispered behind Mary's back as she waddled before them during the days of her pregnancy. It was quite baffling how Joseph the town carpenter could have raised such a wise and knowledgeable Rabbi. "Which rabbinical school did He attend, and when?" They questioned each other, feeling it was their right since they knew Jesus so well.

Phineas invited Jesus to read at the next Sabbath service. Jesus, as always, accepted the invitation offered. He loved His hometown and the people who lived there. He remembered Naomi and her family from next door. The baker and the sandal maker had been childhood friends. They had sat side by side learning their Torah lessons.

It was a bittersweet homecoming for Him. He knew this town was on the road map His Father had drawn up for Him to travel, but that didn't make it any easier. His Heavenly Father had also revealed the rejection He would receive at the very hands of those He called friends.

On the Sabbath Jesus donned His robes, touched the tassels at the hem that reminded Him of His Father's words. A vision of healing came to Him as He touched the tassels pulling His outer robe on. He knew the prophecy He was about to read in their hearing. Isaiah 61 was written inside of Him; the words of the treasured prophet were on Him for He was the fulfillment of them. This truth, He knew, would infuriate the congregation He was about to face, but His secret weapon, His empowerment of His Holy Spirit, emboldened Him to press on and speak the truth in love.

Waypoints to your destination:

From John 4:43-45, what truth did Jesus know as He headed into Nazareth?

Why do you think He continued on into His hometown village?

What intrigue caused Jesus to continue north and leave Samaria?

In Luke 4:14, what was Jesus' secret weapon that strengthened Him to travel on the way to the cross?

"Lord, the same power that took You to Galilee and Your hometown lives in me. God, by the power of Your Holy Spirit and with the wisdom of Your Spirit and with the compassion of Jesus, give me words to speak and ears to listen."

Cana – A City of Miracles

Day Thirty One

"Once more He visited Cana in Galilee, where He had turned water into wine. And there was a certain royal official whose son lay sick at Capernaum. When this man heard that Jesus had arrived in Galilee from Judea, he went to Him and begged Him to come and heal his son, who was close to death" John 4:46-47 NIV.

The halls of heaven's courts echo with parent's intercession. We have prayed over scraped knees, broken bones, shattered hearts, and bruised egos. We cling to the verse, "Because He bends down to listen, I will pray as long as I have breath!" Psalm 116:2 NLT.

There is no sickness too minor that He will not heal. So we call out to God when we see our toddler carted off in a little red wagon for a twenty minute surgery to place ear tubes in a chronically infected ear. Our stomach becomes mush when they wheel our child off to remove the tonsils swollen with bacteria, and we cry out to God for peace.

Then sometimes because of a dire predicament our cries become more than pleas for peace. Drastic times call for drastic measures, and a desperate father runs to The Healer. Despair enters our prayer-life because of a child's sickness and knocks us to our knees. A fever sends us to the pediatrician. Runny noses and listless bodies break our hearts and tumble our thoughts into a chaotic mass of worry.

Unfortunately each of us knows this scenario all too well. It's a fact of life. Children are going to get sick. One moment they are playing and running, skipping and jumping, wrestling and pouncing, then in the next moment you hear the words, "Mom, I don't feel good." The back of your hand reaches out to feel the fevered heat of a brow. This child who was seconds ago active and full of energy, now goes to lie down, and eyes which were bright eyed and bushy tailed now have a fevered glaze shimmering in them.

For the common ear infection or bronchitis or the like, a good round of antibiotics will normally do the trick. Chronic ear infections or strep throat may end in minor surgery with ear tubes or a tonsillectomy, as in my two youngest children, and a couple of my grandsons. It is never the most pleasant of options, but you have faith that the outcome will help your child onto the road of healing. Still, you pray because nothing is too minor for Our Great God.

Other times with hearts breaking parents hear the words, "Pediatric neuroblastoma cancer or Leukemia." Worlds are rocked with that diagnosis. I can't even imagine the fear that envelops and enshrouds their thoughts and hearts. I've personally observed the journeys of some of these parents and I applaud their bravery. I witnessed these parents rush head long into the arms of The Healer, and I can read their story because it is recorded for us in this fourth chapter of John.

This father was a royal official. Maybe he served in Herod's court, or he could have been an official of the Roman government. His prestige does not matter here. Sickness does not distinguish between rich or poor, powerful or lay person. Our planet is contaminated with sickness and disease and one way or another it will infect a part of our life just as it did this official.

This child's illness became more than a worry to this father. This sickness sent him traveling twenty miles away to go see Yeshua. This makes me believe the parents had exhausted all the physicians in Capernaum while day by day the son became more feeble. The father probably could see life draining away from his child and he could stand by no longer. It would have been a day's journey. I'm sure he wouldn't have wanted to leave his son's bedside. I can feel his fear rising in me. "What if? What if I leave and he passes before I return?" I don't think the father wanted to waste any time away from his sick son. This makes me believe this royal official knew this journey would not be a waste. This royal official was at a crossroads. It was his moment of crisis of belief. Stay or go?

"When he heard that Jesus had come out of Judea into Galilee, he went to Him..." John 4:47 NKJV.

From the moment Jesus stepped foot into Galilee the Galileans accepted Him. The masses followed Him. Whole villages had witnessed His miracles in Jerusalem, and their belief and stories inspired hope into this father who was facing a hopeless situation.

That's the fact of faith. Faith replaces despair. Maybe the father's steps toward Jesus were small and slow at first, but still he went to a place of hope. Jesus was in Cana where just a few months earlier He had turned water into wine. Cana was the beginning place where legends were made (at least for Jesus that is.) The story of this miracle spread throughout the countryside and it made its way into Capernaum where this royal official lived. Maybe at first he paid no attention, but when the rubber met the road and he faced an impossible situation, in his desperation, the story of this miracle and many more became a lifesaver of hope.

He was about to lose his son. His heart lay broken and pouring out with fear. This father put reputation aside and approached Jesus. He even went so far as to beg. He implored Jesus to come to Capernaum and heal his son. His faith was faulty. He believed Jesus had to be in his son's presence to heal. Faulty faith does not matter to Jesus. Sincere faith is what is required and desperate faith moved Him. Jesus was not about to turn this father away during his crisis. His very nature of compassion would not allow Him. The father's grief appealed to Him. Again, we see Jesus shifting gears because of cries for help. When invitations were offered Jesus accepted.

Verse 48 of John 4 is a lament of Jesus'. "Unless you people see signs and wonders, you will by no means believe." He knew what was in this father's heart and in the crowd's that stood around Him. He was trying to move them from shallow faith to a deeper faith. They needed a faith that would steady them through the winds of sickness. This father was so moved.

"Sir, come down before my child dies!" John 4:49 NKJV.

The father would not relent in his request. He held onto Jesus like a bull rider in the arena. Jesus did not hold his ignorance against him for with His next breath He spoke life and health into this father's situation and into his son.

"Jesus said to him, "Go your way; your son lives" John 4:50 NKJV.

When Jesus spoke, power went out of Him. It was a power to heal across time and space and it was a power that embedded confident faith in the father. At that moment Jesus' words reached out across the twenty miles and brought life where death had once resided.

"So the man believed the word that Jesus spoke to him, and he went his way" John 4:50 NKJV.

At Jesus' words the father turned to retrace his steps to his son whom he loved. He let loose of Jesus and in faith faced the unknown of returning to a place where the shadow of death had once consumed his life. That is the power of The Word. Jesus' promise moved the father to accept.

"And as he was now going down, his servants met him and told him, saying, "Your son lives! Then he inquired of them the hour when he got better. "Yesterday at the seventh hour the fever left him." So the father knew that it was at the same hour in which Jesus said to him, "Your son lives." And he himself believed, and his whole household" John 4:51-53 NKJV.

The words of Jesus led the father into faith and belief one step at a time. They took him deeper and deeper to a rock solid foundation. The father faced a hopeless sickness, this led him to seek Jesus. When he came face to face with The Healer, he begged and implored. He bared all his heartache before Jesus and he did not let anything push him off this path. He invited Jesus into his world of pain. Then when he heard the words of promise, he stopped his begging and being confident of the words, turned to confront his situation. There were steps he had to take between the time of the promise given till the time of the promise fulfilled. Only then did he get confirmation of the promise.

He had wrong assumptions about the healing. He didn't fully grasp the power of Jesus. He assumed his son's healing would be gradual, but his servants knew first-hand the full weight of this healing. The son's fever was completely gone. Wrong assumptions did not nor could not subtract from the power of God. The father's faith became confirmed faith which became contagious faith.

Jesus still leads us to climb those same stairs of faith. Disease touches all of us in some form or fashion, through a family member or a friend or even you personally. We would rather run from it but sometimes you just can't. It may keep you up all night. You might have to rock your child while breathing your warm breath into an ear that is bursting with pain. It may send you to St. Jude's Children's hospital to seek treatments for your child with leukemia.

It's not fair and it's not pretty, but disease can never be the champion when you have that intimate relationship with The Healer. Those who are in Christ have that certain hope and a special footing with the One who is greater than sickness, disease, and cancer. His heart aches over our pain. He collects our tears and sheds his own, and His halls vibrate with our cries for healing.

I have seen the steps of this father's confident faith written into the lives of dear friends. A diagnosis of leukemia had been pronounced over their little one. They came to Jesus begging and imploring. They invited Him into their brokenness. They too received words of life, "Your daughter will be healed," and they too turned to bravely face what lay ahead for them knowing that Jesus loved their little girl. A confident faith like this becomes a contagious faith for friends, family, and towns. We need to let our stories of Jesus spread out across the countryside. We overcome all things by the blood of the Lamb and by the word of our testimony.

Off to See The Healer
Yaash stood in the doorframe feeling helpless. A lone tear slid down his cheek. He didn't think he could have any more

tears left. His wife, Jarush, wiped the cool cloth across their son's brow. Benani lay there with ragged breath. He was fighting, that was for sure. Yaash could hear as the boy labored for air to fill his lungs.

Physicians had traipsed in and out of their home for days. Each time they left with only a slight shake of their head. Yaash could see it in their countenance. There was nothing they could do. These physicians did not have the ability to breathe life into his son. With each shallow breath the boy took, Yaash could feel his own breath being knocked out of him. He had nothing left. Despair was like a heavy cloak of iron chains pulling him deep into the dark abyss.

Yaash clenched his fist and thrust it into the wall leaving a gaping hole behind. The situation was out of his control and he could not bear the helplessness he felt. Through the halls he could hear the whisperings of the servants. Yaash knew they loved Benani also. The boy was such a charmer and had been so active and mischievous. He had brought such joy into this home.

For a moment Yaash focused on the servants' conversation. He heard the name, Yeshua. What about that name? Why was it so familiar? He summoned Ebed to inquire of the murmurings of the staff. Ebed reminded him of Yeshua's ability to turn water into wine, and told Yaash how most of Galilee had seen the new Rabbi perform one type of miracle or another. Then Ebed told Yaash that Yeshua was in Cana.

"Grab my cloak. You stay behind and watch over my boy. I am going to Cana." Yaash set out. He could do nothing at home, but he could do this.

He pushed past his fears of death, kissed his wife and held his child. "Would this be his last hug?" Yaash wondered to himself. This time he would not allow himself to tumble down that hole. Finally, he felt hope rising as he walked the road to

Cana. "Yeshua, was He myth or legend?" Yaash wondered as he journeyed on. Something in him knew that at the end of this road he would find A Great Physician. Yaash couldn't clarify his thoughts for they were an unknown call to faith. This faith was spoken into him from the Father who created him. This road of faith beckoned to Yaash, and Cana became a shining city on the hill glowing from the Presence of the Light of the World. Cana would be his miracle city. Yaash was certain of it.

Waypoints to your destination:

How did Jesus respond to the father's pleas?

How did Jesus heal the boy?

Describe a time you felt you were in a hopeless situation.

What did you do?

"Lord God, great and awesome are You. I praise you because there is nothing so minor You will not touch and nothing so major You cannot heal. God Almighty, You've got this."

The Walk of the Tortured

Day Thirty Two

"Then they went into Capernaum, and right away He entered the synagogue on the Sabbath and began to teach. They were astonished at His teaching because, unlike the scribes, He was teaching them as one having authority. Just then a man with an unclean spirit was in their synagogue. He cried out, "What do You have to do with us, Jesus – Nazarene? Have You come to destroy us? I know who You are – the Holy One of God!" But Jesus rebuked him and said, "Be quiet, and come out of him!" And the unclean spirit convulsed him, shouted with a loud voice, and came out of him" Mark 1:21-26 HCSB.

"Then they were all amazed, so they began to argue with one another, saying, "What is this? A new teaching with authority! He commands even the unclean spirits, and they obey Him." News about Him then spread throughout the entire vicinity of Galilee" Mark 1:27- 28 HCSB.

"Poor Charlie." This is always my thought as I watch Landry put a muzzle on Charlie so that he can take Charlie for a walk. Charlie is my 150 pound bull mastiff grand dog. He's a beastly looking dog with a tender heart, except... Except when other dogs invade his personal bubble or the personal space of his master, my son Landry, or the personal space of our little prince, my grandson Ezekiel Matthew Jones. When those events occur Charlie has been known to nonchalantly place a paw on the unsuspecting dog's head and bite down. Due to the way Charlie has been created, when Charlie closes in on the bite, his jaws lock down and there is no escaping those jowls. It's not his fault really. Charlie has a very laid-back disposition, except when certain people's personal space seems to get invaded.

Thus, the muzzle is necessary. It's a contraption straight out of a Hollywood horror movie. Nightmares are forged from the sight of Charlie's muzzle. I choose not to look as Charlie obediently traipses down the sidewalk following his master all the while looking like a canine Hannibal Lector. Charlie gets muzzled for his own good, and for the safety of other dogs who might accidentally cross his walking path. Landry is exercising his authority over his pet, controlling the pent up anxiety of Charlie, and Charlie succumbs in obedience to his loving master.

"What has Charlie's muzzle got to do with these verses in Mark?" You might ask. The picture of Landry muzzling Charlie is exactly what Jesus did to the evil spirit who possessed the man in the synagogue. Jesus exercised His authority over evil spirits, muzzled the spirit, and closed the spirit's mouth so that it couldn't open. Jesus took away the spirit's ability to talk and then He commanded the spirit to come out of the man. Landry's muzzle over Charlie's mouth affords Landry the freedom to walk Charlie. He knows Charlie can't open his mouth and cause harm. The muzzle allows Landry to command Charlie and guide him down the sidewalks of Mt. Lebanon, PA.

Let's turn back the clock and set the scene to grasp the full impact of the authority Jesus has over the physical, spiritual and mental capacities of human beings and the world in which we live.

Jesus had just returned to the region of Galilee. He had been rejected in His hometown of Nazareth, but that did not detour Him from following on down the path His Father had prepared for Him. It was a downhill jaunt from Nazareth. Word of His fame spread like the flames of a wildfire. A government official stopped Him in Cana, begging Jesus to heal his son. We saw that Jesus had authority over time and space. He didn't have to be present with the child. His Word and command traveled the distance between Cana and Capernaum. The official's son was healed completely. Can you imagine the buzz that event created among the villagers of Capernaum?

Jesus, James, John, Simon, Andrew, Nathanael, and Philip, had just traveled down an important road that connected the port of Ptolemaic to Cana, from Cana to Magdala for six miles, and from there northeast to Capernaum for another six miles. They passed through green olive groves to get to the Sea of Galilee. These first six disciples were back home. The familiar smell of the sea and fish were the aromas of comfort to them. Capernaum, the place of family and friends, welcomed this traveling band. The news of Jesus' arrival echoed across the shores of the sea.

As was His custom, Jesus entered the synagogue and began to teach. He didn't stop at go, He didn't do a meet and greet, no platitudes and gratitude, the moment Jesus set foot in the village of Capernaum, He began teaching in the synagogue. Synagogue's were often used as a school or even a general gathering place. They were the center of society for most Jewish villages. People assembled for services not only on Sabbath but on Mondays and Thursdays as well, and because Jesus was a faithful Jewish Rabbi and the obedient Son of God, He honored the Sabbath and kept it holy.

A synagogue was not the place of sacrifice. That was the temple in Jerusalem. A synagogue was a place of worship, prayer and reading the law and the prophets. Jesus had freedom to minister in these because each synagogue was led by laymen and not priests.

On this day when Jesus taught God's Word in this synagogue, He had probably been invited by the synagogue ruler in Capernaum. Before He even showed His power, Jesus' words evoked a catalyst in His listeners.

Teachers of the Law in Jesus' day were schooled in written law and oral interpretation of that law by whatever Rabbi they sat under. When they taught they were often quoting the sayings of their master to make their point. It was a sermon of rote quibbling and quotations. Have you ever heard the saying, "A dry sermon?" It's a sermon that doesn't move you to make a change in your life. This was the type of monotone teaching to which the people were accustomed. This was why there was such astonishment among the worshipers when Jesus spoke.

His was a new teaching that had the power to move and create emotion and change in them. It was forthright, confident, and authoritative. Jesus spoke with the power of God's Spirit. He had creative ability in His words, His tone, and His voice. His teachings were edgy, and were not tethered by references to other Rabbis. He spoke because He had come from God His Father, the Creator of the universe.

His words had the power to bring what was unseen to the forefront. On this day Jesus' presence and authority provoked a strong outburst from a man under the control of an evil spirit. Having a fear of Jesus, this demon set out to disrupt worship and confuse the congregation. The demon wanted to get the attention onto himself and off of Jesus, but

Jesus took control of the situation. He didn't use the incantations of exorcists. With just a few direct words, "Be muzzled," the evil spirit released control of the service over to Jesus. The demon violently exited the man striving to leave destruction in its wake, but Luke 4:35 from HCSB says, "And throwing him down before them, the demon came out of him without hurting him at all." Jesus maintained total control over the situation and of this demon. He completely delivered this poor tortured soul while exercising His power to protect him in the process.

We read the account of Jesus driving out an unclean spirit from our side of His-story. We know Jesus is the Son of God. This congregation did not have that luxury. The people were just beginning to grasp this Rabbi's authority. From their side of history it was a slow revelation. The demons knew who He was. They were there when Jesus expelled them from heaven. Jesus wasn't about to let His true identity be revealed by His enemies. His creation must come to belief in Him through His own words and actions.

Jesus' travels were far from peaceful. Corporate worship with Jesus was plagued by raucous behavior. Can you imagine the stir it would cause if something like that were to happen in your next worship experience? All of Tulsa would be ablaze with the talk.

Landry walks Charlie with a muzzle because as Charlie's owner, Landry has that prerogative. Landry is able to control the walk with Charlie's muzzle in place. He is exercising his authority as Charlie's master. Jesus was exercising His authority over spiritual matters on this day. He placed a muzzle over the mouth of an evil spirit. The control of worship was in Jesus' hands. Jesus' authority and the power of His commands protected this man from that which wanted to cause harm. His words contained weight and power, and they made things happen.

Only Jesus has the power to liberate us from things that enslave us. Only Jesus has the words that will muzzle all fears and worries, and things that go bump in the night.

Muzzling a Demon

Chemah rode his person hard often using a spiked whip to incite the rage on his unsuspecting transport. Agno had no idea when Chemah entered his being. He had left a door of anger open and Chemah walked right through. Chemah lived up to his name. This evil spirit could provoke rage in Agno through as simple an annoyance as a slamming door. Chemah's sadistic influence threw Agno into bouts of temper tantrums. Agno's family knew to seek cover the moment his voice would hint of an unknown hysteria.

Agno was ignorant of his rider. All Agno knew was the rising heat and the profound itch inside of him. He couldn't control his outbursts. At times he wanted to rip at his own skin as if he could turn himself inside out. An eerie voice inside his thoughts enticed him to throw scalding water through his kitchen. The voice reconciled Agno's action with thoughts of deservedness. Agno was the innocent; it was everyone else who was in the wrong.

Oh, he had times of lucidness and clarity often going days and weeks without an incident. Then, out of the blue, rage would well up in his soul. Agno could no longer contain it. It was as if a pressure valve had defaulted and the steam inside had to vent. Chemah would rub his hands with their razor sharp nails with glee. His nails dripped with gangrenous ooze because Chemah had just ripped into Agno's spirit with nails laced with poisonous rage.

Thus was their life together, Agno and his demonic rider. Until the day Yeshua entered in. It was one of those clear lucid days. Agno was in his right mind as he wandered the wharfs of Capernaum. He was fixing fresh fish for dinner tonight. He went to Zebedee's boat to purchase the fresh fish which they had caught the night before. The synagogue loomed before him. Agno was a member and often times Chemah had allowed Agno to participate in synagogue worship. Chemah knew religion, rote readings and the teachings of Moses' law would not change Agno, so he allowed this habit.

This day was different though. Demon and human could sense it. The crowd had overflowed the volume level of the synagogue. A new Rabbi was in town and was teaching. Agno drew closer to investigate and pushed through the crowd with the force Chemah possessed. The Voice, His Tone, and His Words began a sharp slicing pain in Chemah's ears. He had heard this Voice before during the great battle between Lucifer and his demonic horde and the Son of God and His angelic army. The pain in Chemah's ears reverberated down his spine. He screeched with all the energy he could muster, "Jesus of Nazareth! What do you want with us? Did you come to destroy us? I know who you are – God's Holy One!" Chemah's nails and hands were ripping into Agno's ear lobes. He must shut off the Voice. He could not allow it to enter Agno's spirit.

"Be quiet! Come out of the man!" Seven simple words, one powerful command and Chemah was muzzled. No more cancerous words would ooze out of his fowl mouth. Gone was the tempestuous inflictions that incited rage. Chemah's mouth was clamped shut by the muzzle of the Word of God. This muzzle was a steel trap anchored down with iron spikes. Now, it was Chemah's turn to fly into a rage as he squirmed and tried to pry out of the steel contraption. He broke his own jawbone

trying to escape this prison. Chemah slammed his unsuspecting transport onto the rock hard floor of the synagogue. Thrashing Agno about, Chemah himself writhing in pain. Letting out the scream of a banshee, he slithered out of Agno. Turning, hoping to find destruction in his wake, Chemah saw Agno sitting on the pew with a look of deep gratitude gleaming in his eye. "Lucifer will not be happy about this," Chemah moaned and prepared himself for another beating.

Waypoints to your destination:

What was the people's reaction to Jesus' teaching?

What do you think was different about the way Jesus taught?

What was the evidence of Jesus' authority?

What are your thoughts about the power Jesus possesses, and do you think His power applies to you today?

"Lord, You alone have the power to muzzle all the evil influences that have come to disrupt my walk with You. Hold my hand and speak Your commands into my heart, soul, mind and strength."

A Mile in His Sandals

Day Thirty Three

"As soon as Jesus and His followers left the synagogue, they went with James and John to the home of Simon and Andrew. Simon's mother-in-law was sick in bed with a fever, and the people told Jesus about her. So Jesus went to her bed, took her hand, and helped her up. The fever left her, and she began serving them.

That evening, after the sun went down, the people brought to Jesus all who were sick and had demons in them. The whole town gathered at the door. Jesus healed many who had different kinds of sicknesses and He forced many demons to leave people. But He would not allow the demons to speak, because they knew who He was. Early the next morning, while it was still dark, Jesus woke and left the house. He went to a lonely place, where He prayed" Mark 1:29-35 NCV.

I felt my I-watch alarm vibrate against my wrist. "Ugh! It can't be already. Six thirty came way to fast this morning." I touched the stop button on the alarm as I mentally went through my to-do list. It was packing day. Tomorrow I would be leaving for Addis Ababa Ethiopia and I had much to do on this day. "Okay, I deserve a sleep in day." I reasoned with myself. For the next week and a half I was going to be up early and going all day as I served and visited the people in Addis. When I landed back home in America, I would go immediately to Pittsburgh and take care of my grandson for the weekend. I gauged each day by how much rest I would get throughout my next couple of weeks. "Yep," I determined I deserve this. I took off my I-watch and rolled over and slept for three more hours, skipping my morning quiet time with the Lord.

It is called "the to-do list," and it is demanding. It robs us of our rest and keeps us from propping our feet up and just taking a breather. At times our "to-do" list becomes so overwhelming that we become irritable. It can steal our peace. How do we tame it? How can we become the master and not allow it to master us? How did Jesus do it?

I took a look at a single day in the life of our Lord and it exhausted me. To walk a mile in His sandals would require great energy. In one 24 hour period He drove out an unclean spirit from a man at church, went to a friend's house for lunch, healed His friend's mother-in-law, ate lunch and had communion with His friends, and then as the sun set, He opened the door and saw the whole town of Capernaum gathered at the doorstep. Well into the night, He healed the sick and drove out demons. It had to have been late when Jesus finally had a chance to take a break and lay down His head, but did He sleep in after a demanding day of healing? No, early the next morning while it was still dark, Jesus headed out to pray.

Jesus' Sabbath was hectic to say the least. There was no Sunday afternoon nap. Every single moment was spent engaged in the lives of the people He came to save. He went to lunch as a guest to Simon but soon became the host of Simon's house. He constantly gave of himself. Jesus poured His energy and love into a world in need. He was on a mission and time was growing short.

He also allowed people to fill His need. He was the itinerate pastor and there was nowhere else for Him to go for lunch. Simon and Andrew filled that need and invited Jesus and His followers to their home to eat. They didn't leave Jesus at church, instead they took Him home and invited Him into their lives after Sunday morning church. They asked Him to share in their Monday thru Saturday blessings and burdens.

Simon's mother-in-law lay sick with a fever. I recently had the stomach flu and ran 102 fever. Literally, it hurt to raise my head off the pillow. I was in no shape to entertain guests, neither did I want to. Kevin would slightly open the door to my darkened room and check on my well-being. I would grunt out, "I feel horrible and I'm running fever. Don't bother me." In the next minute I was texting him, "Could you please go get me some tea?" I'm a mother-in-law and I was recently sick in bed with a fever, "Yeah, my story is written out in the Word of God." These verses had me sitting up and taking notes.

Jesus entered Simon's house to be fed but the moment a sickness confronted Him, He gave compassion. His need was put on the back burner. Mercy and the Father's love drove His every movement. Three simple actions were all that was required of Him. He didn't shy away from someone running a fever. They say you are the most contagious while you are running a fever. Jesus put all worry aside and went to Simon's mother-in-law's bedside. He gave her the gift of touch, took her by the hand and helped her to stand. In that moment of touch a power went out of Him and the mother-in-law was healed. The healing power of Jesus became personal to Simon and Andrew right then. The Great Physician had just walked into their home and into their family's lives.

The fever left her immediately at the touch of the Master. It took me a week to gain back my energy after I had this bout with the flu, but at His touch she got up and began serving this band of brothers. The fever should have left her in a weakened condition, but Jesus' healing was complete and it filled her with strength enough to serve. It was a healing performed in private, and broke the strictest teaching of the Pharisees, "No work will be done on the Sabbath," but it fulfilled God's law of mercy and compassion.

The healing of Simon's mother-in-law was just a snapshot of this event filled Sabbath. As was usually the case, Jesus' private healings led to public healings. When the sun set on this Sabbath the sick came calling.

There was no chance to go to the roof and catch His breath, and maybe lie down a few moments. The guest of the house went to the front porch and became The Great Physician to the masses.

Ten miles from Capernaum were the healing hot mineral waters of Tiberius. These mineral baths were the center of one of the most famous spas of the day. They were known to have curative properties. The sick and ailing traveled from afar to dip themselves into these healing waters, but on this day they forgo the baths and went and sat upon Simon's doorstep. Mark's gospel says, "The whole town gathered at the door" Mark 1:32 NCV. In the middle of a great health resort area, the Great Physician healed the ailments of the multitudes.

The Bible doesn't say how long Jesus labored that evening. All we know is He began after sunset and He healed many and forced many demons to leave the people. He didn't get in His Sunday after church, lie on the couch for an entire two hours, type of nap. Compassion drove Him, and doing the will of His Father was His strength, so He pushed through the night. The ER that once was full and overflowing, one by one emptied as He did the triage of His Father.

How was He not drained? How was He not completely emptied out on behalf of all those He touched? He served the masses. He heard their stories. His heart broke. When He closed His eyes that night, did He see, hear, and feel their pain? Did He fall upon His mat exhausted?

Yet, "Early the next morning, while it was still dark, Jesus woke and left the house. He went to a lonely place, where He prayed" Mark 1:35 NCV. He didn't hit the snooze alarm. Jesus didn't reason that He deserved a sleep in day after the busy Sunday He had. "While it was still dark..." Jesus went to a solitary place so He could pray and have communion with His Father. Even though Sunday was hectic, Jesus got ready for Monday and the coming week's activities by having His quiet time with God. He didn't forgo that time. He gained strength from His time spent with God.

That day in the life of Jesus, Jesus had a large "to-do list", but He turned it into a "to-love list" as Ann Voskamp would say. Through His acts of love, mercy and healing, Jesus found a strength that was beyond His physical man. He emptied Himself. "He made Himself nothing by taking the very nature of a servant, being made in human likeness" Philippians 2:7 NIV. The interests of the masses wooed Him to serve and heal. He may have looked like a man, but His acts of love became a window through which the people saw the love of a great God and the healing of the Great Physician.

A study has shown that little acts of love and serving others releases dopamine in your brain. Dopamine is the hormone associated with positive emotions and a natural high. I know it is counterintuitive to what we believe to be true. In my mind I believe I require great rest after service to my fellow man. I deserve a sleep in day and God will understand if I miss an appointment or two.

I had all my kids under my roof during a rare weekend. I cooked three meals a day. It was a veritable smorgasbord. They left, my house was quiet and I told my husband I was boycotting cooking for a while. I deserved a break.

Jesus sets a different model. In serving and giving He lived life abundantly. Time spent with God infused Him with energy to face His hectic lifestyle. I don't know that I could walk a mile in His sandals. I'm spent just reading about His exploits on this Sabbath day, but what seems counterintuitive to me actually does fill me with energy to face each and every day with grace.

It's like the little electric car I came across the other day. I had to laugh. It was so cute charging up at its charging station. While it was getting charged up so that it would have the power to drive on down the road, it's owner was eating her lunch inside the car. She was getting her fuel so she could travel on through the rest of her day. It occurred to me, that is the exact picture of Jesus on this day. These acts of healing and mercy gave Him the adrenaline rush He needed to push through the night. Getting up early to be with His Heavenly Father was like that charging station for that little electric car.

"My food," said Jesus, "is to do the will of Him who sent me and to finish His work" John 4:34 NIV.

If I want to live that abundant life Jesus promises, I must follow His example. Empty myself out and serve my fellow man in the capacity the Lord has placed inside of me. Once emptied, I must be filled again. That filling must come from moments spent in the presence of the Lord Most High. Only He can infuse us with the energy of His Holy Spirit that we might fulfill His purpose for us as we follow Jesus on the way to eternity.

His Touch

Naomi lay there upon her bed. Her strength was drained. She hated this part of the sickness. This fever had touched her life upon multiple occasions, but this time was different. Her limbs felt like lead weighing her down plastering her to the mat. The headache was the worst. The room spun each time she lifted it. She knew her beloved daughter Ruth fretted over her. Even her son-in-law Simon cast worried glances her way. He was a faithful son-in-law and took good care of her since she had become a widow.

Simon had recently returned to Capernaum recanting stories of a new Rabbi who had the power to heal. Yeshua was guest speaking at the synagogue this Sabbath. Naomi desired nothing more than to go to the synagogue with her family. If only He would heal her and break this blasted fever that was zapping her very life.

Lying there with chills running up and down her spine, she felt as if she was in a fog. Muffled voices barely penetrated her conscience. She gave in to the heat of the fever and sickness. Delirium would set in soon. It would be a welcome state compared to the pain in her body, but then the hairs on her arm prickled as if an electric current was passing through her body. She felt a touch like no other she had experienced in her life. Her eyes fluttered open for the first time in weeks.

Naomi looked into eyes filled with compassion. He came. Though she had never met this man named Yeshua, she knew Him. This was the Healer. No other had the power He exuded when He clasped her hand. He touched her. He stood Naomi to her feet.

Naomi did not swoon. There was no faltering in her step. An otherworldly energy infused her being by His touch. Joy flooded her soul. Overwhelming thankfulness now drove her to serve Him. Something happened to her because He touched her. The hand of Yeshua, the Great Physician, stood her up. Naomi left her sick bed behind and now she served because He had made her whole.

Waypoints to your destination:

What actions did Jesus take in Mark 1:31?

What do you think it might have felt like when Jesus touched Simon's mother-in-law?

What happened after sunset?

Where do you think Jesus got the energy for this full day of service?

"Lord, infuse me with this energy. Lord, may I never neglect my time with You. You are my energy supply. You have touched me and made me whole and I thank you."

Deep Waters

Day Thirty Four

"As the crowd was pressing in on Jesus to hear God's word, He was standing by Lake Gennesaret. He saw two boats at the edge of the lake; the fishermen had left them and were washing their nets. He got into one of the boats, which belonged to Simon, and asked him to put out a little from the land. Then He sat down and was teaching the crowds from the boat" Luke 5:1-3 HCSB.

I sat in her fifteen by six foot shack with its tarp lined mud walls and just listened. Zacharias was speaking to her in her native tongue, Amharic. Zacharias is around thirteen and is an orphan who lives in one of the homes of IAMNOT4GOTTEN. He's lived a life of grief and pain, filled with hunger and neglect while he lived on the streets of Addis Ababa Ethiopia as early as six years of age. Zacharias asked Jesus to be his Savior when he came to live with IAMNOT4GOTTEN Ministries.

Now, just a few short years later here he sat giving his testimony and explaining to this young momma that God never wastes our trials. This precious child of God identified with her suffering. We learned she carries her six year old daughter with Spina Bifida two hours to and from school. This young mother makes what she can earning a living for her and her daughter by taking in laundry. Her life is filled with hardships also.

We all sat on her only piece of furniture, a rickety wood bed she shared with Blaine, her daughter. All the while Zacharias spoke, I debated with God. "What am I doing here?" "I know nothing of her deep suffering."

At his young age, Zacharias, had seen and experienced more heartache than I could imagine. I was seven thousand miles from the comfort of my home and I couldn't figure out why I was here.

Tears were flowing and I was confused. I felt like I was in deep waters without a life saver. My Titanic had just capsized and I was floating on driftwood in the Atlantic Ocean that I had just crossed. I felt unproductive and useless on this trip. I had cast my fishing net and it had returned to me void.

As I argued, God threw me my life vest. "I have made them Fishers of Men," I heard Him whisper to my heart. Since we began the ministry of IAMNOT4GOTTEN, I had been praying that God would take these young men and teach them how to spread the Gospel of Christ to their country. Peace washed away my arguments. I was here because God let me see His answer to my prayers.

One by one as I heard the accounts of our trip, God affirmed this to me. The boys in our homes were going out into their country and telling what God had done in their lives. God had called several to become fishers of men and they were telling their stories. They were relating to the hardships of their fellow countrymen. God was just allowing me to witness His work in their lives and His answers to my prayers.

The boys of IAMNOT4GOTTEN have nothing, but on this trip Jesus used them, just as He used Simon's fishing boat. On this day walking the shores of the Sea of Galilee, the people were pressing into Him. They were invading His personal space and they were pushing Him into the waters.

He had been in their area and had performed many miracles. He had healed Simon's mother-in-law of a terrible fever and He had set up an urgent care on Simon's doorstep. The whole town of Capernaum camped out in Simon's front yard and Jesus had healed them one by one.

Now they wanted more and they pressed Him for it. The crowd was imposing and demanding, but Jesus allowed them to break into His walk. He had a great need because He was about to be pushed in the water. He saw an ordinary fishing boat and He climbed aboard.

The boat just happened to belong to His friend Simon. They had a pre-existing relationship. Simon had been with Him since John the Baptist had said, "Look the Lamb of God..." Simon had followed Jesus to Jerusalem, through the hills of Judea and the wells of Samaria. The healing of his mother-in-law had made Jesus' miracles personal to Him. Now Jesus needed something from him and He obliged. "Put out a little from land," Jesus asked Simon. Up until now their relationship had just been building, but now Jesus enters Simon's workspace.

His words carried across the ripples of the sea. The crowd was like sheep without a shepherd and they drank in His teachings. Their souls were precious to Him. He came to bring them good news. Jesus, friend of sinners, came to their city to seek and to save. The backdrop of His preaching was the fish smelling shores of the Sea of Galilee. Jesus took His Words into their world. His platform was an ordinary fishing boat. He used what was at hand.

"When He had finished speaking, He said to Simon, "Put out into deep water and let down your nets for a catch."

Master," Simon replied, "we've worked hard all night long and caught nothing! But at Your word, I'll let down the nets." When they did this, they caught a great number of fish, and their nets began to tear. So they signaled to their partners in the other boat to come and help them; they came and filled both boats so full that they began to sink" Luke 5:4-7 HCSB.

Simon and Andrew, John and James had toiled all night and had nothing to show for their hard work. Jesus knew their lack of success from the previous night. On the heels of Simon's most unproductive business night, Jesus entered into their everyday work life and because of Jesus they had the most productive business day of their careers. A carpenter showed professional fishermen where the fish were. It was as if Jesus had sonar built into His brain.

The first command, "Put out a little..." was the first ripple in the water. Simon obeyed. The relationship between Teacher and student had already been established. Jesus' miracles had entered Simon's family life and now they were entering his work place.

Simon obeyed the first simple command even though he was exhausted from the night before. He sat and was a captive audience to some charismatic preaching, but the second command was a little tougher to swallow. "Put out into deep water..." The shallows are where the fish are. Every Galilean fisherman knew this. Deep water was unchartered territory for Simon, and contrary to his training and his expertise.

These are the steps of faith. "Put out a little..." We are to hear the words of Christ, and then launch out into deep water. Simon had to obey the first command and take another step of obedience, go out into the unknown, before he could experience the miracle that changed his unproductive business venture. He went from nothing to an overabundance that nearly sank his fishing fleet. It was as if a whole new fishery had opened up on the sea floor.

Simon's fishing net enclosed around a great catch of fish, so much so that his nets were breaking. He and his team had hit the jackpot. It was the climax of this story and Simon could do nothing but fall to his knees.

"When Simon Peter saw this, he fell at Jesus' knees and said, "Go away from me, because I'm a sinful man, Lord!" For he and all those with him were amazed at the catch of fish they took, and so were Simon's partners."

"Don't be afraid," Jesus told Simon. "From now on you will be catching people!" Then they brought the boats to land, left everything, and followed Him" Luke 5:1-11 HCSB.

Simon came face to face with a man who had the ability to see unseen riches. Simon sensed he was in the presence of holiness, and all else faded. The crowds were at the shore, his brother and partners looked on, but for this moment it was Jesus and him. Simon realized his own inadequacy and unholiness. Amazement and fear fused together in one emotion. Andrew, James, and John became engulfed in the same set of emotions swirling around. Jesus entered their personal workspace. They experienced His power tangibly in their own lives and because they did they left everything to follow Jesus.

When Jesus becomes real and His work in your life is personal, you too will leave everything and follow Him.

Jesus used what was at hand. Simon's boat became His pulpit. That day in Ethiopia, God used one who was available to Him. A young teenage boy became God's mouthpiece.

Only God can bring abundance and productivity into our everyday lives. All He asks of us is diligence and obedience. Simon and his partners were diligent in their business but they were often disappointed, but in walks the Man from Galilee, a carpenter's Son, and their life was never the same again.

My grandson Lucas chose his Aunt Whitney to be his fishing partner for the night. They sat there side by side in the dark, fishing off the dock, aunt and nephew just talking about the eeriness of the black night. "Hey Aunt Whitney, I think there is something on my line." Lucas told her. At first Whitney dismissed his claim. She helped Lucas reel in his line and as the squirming fish broke the plane of the water, aunt and nephew squealed calling for help. PopPop had told them it's best to fish at night in the coolness. He instructed Lucas to let his line drop all the way to the lake bottom and then reel it up some. "Fish are swimming down where the waters are cooler." Sometimes you have to take good advice if you want to be productive.

Deep waters, dark lakes, and unknown futures, are terrifying. They can leave us paralyzed with fear and we become unproductive in our journey through life. We may even believe we are beyond saving, but then enters Jesus, and He makes miracles happen in deep water. He is the author and perfector of our faith. His work in our life becomes personal and we own it. He is with us in the deep waters and our lives become filled with productivity. We become "Fishers of men."

Put out into deep water
The muscles in his neck ached from the long night of hauling nothing but net. With each cast and subsequent haul the nets came back empty and their hope drained in the void. Simon leaned over his dirty fishing nets. There was no smell of fish on them this morning. He was tired, weary, and

disappointed. *Cleaning these nets were a drudgery knowing they had nothing to take to market and nothing to show for their hard work. Andrew, John, and James had the same downcast countenance as he had.*

Simon saw the Miracle Worker strolling the shores of the sea. The people were closing in like vultures, pressing into Jesus almost pushing Him out into the water. Simon watched as Jesus climbed into the first thing available to Him. It was his boat, the boat that had just hauled in nothing but net. Melancholy had settled into his bones, never the less, Simon went to the Teacher, to give Him aid.

Jesus had need of a pulpit to speak to the sea of people. Simon had the skills and the boat that would steady the Rabbi as He spoke. "Put out a little," Jesus requested of him. His triceps burned with each row of the paddle. Jesus' words were spoken loud and true, and Simon was a captive audience to the power that rang out from Jesus. For a moment Simon was lost in the sermon. For a moment he forgot the emptiness of the night before.

Then Jesus focused all His attention on Simon. "Put out into the deep," He commanded. The futile night merged into the Words of Jesus, "Teacher, we toiled all night and caught nothing! But at Your word, I'll let down the nets." Hopelessness merged with hope and both warred inside Simon.

At once a great school of fish swam into the net. The net enclosed around a catch so heavy its rope began to unravel. Seeing their nets tearing Simon had Andrew signal for their partners, James and John. Knowing how sound travels across the waters, they didn't want to alert any competitors to their jack pot. Both boats became filled to capacity and beyond.

Who was this carpenter? He had discovered a new spring of fish that had opened in the floor of the lake. To Simon, Jesus was the Rain Man. Here was a guy that had the knowledge to help them become wealthy overnight. Simon had traveled with Him for months now. Jesus was a penniless Rabbi who didn't own a bed. He was a wandering gypsy who taught people for nothing. In that moment Jesus became holy to him. He saw the only thing that mattered to Jesus was the sea of people gathered on the shore. To Jesus, they were the Great Catch.

With this miraculous catch of fish, Jesus became more than Rabbi, Jesus became his Lord. Simon fell at Jesus' knees recognizing the dirt and grime of his worldly life. He was so unworthy of this Man's help, Simon couldn't lift his head to Jesus. The Rabbi from Galilee had taken his unproductive life and had broken into it with abundance. Jesus of Nazareth deserved his all and nothing less.

Simon, Andrew, James and John left the miraculous catch of fish with their families. They would sell them at market and reap an abundant profit. Jesus had provided for the families of these fishermen. The four men walked off into an unknown future knowing that Jesus would take care of those they left behind. They put out into deep water with the One who knows what lies beyond the sea. Jesus would use their skill set and their diligence. He would make them Fishers of Men.

Waypoints to your destination:

How do you think these fishermen felt after a night with nothing to show for their efforts?

What miracle did Jesus give to the fisherman?

Have you ever felt like you were treading in deep water?

Has Jesus ever showed up in your deep water?

"Lord, only You can take an unproductive life and turn it into abundance. Use me. Thank you that You are with us in deep waters. Give me courage to follow You into unchartered waters. Make me a Fisher of Men."

Up on the House Top

Day Thirty Five

"Then everyone was astounded, and they were giving glory to God. And they were filled with awe and said, "We have seen incredible things today!" Luke 5:26 HCSB.

"Up on the house top, click, click, click, down through the chimney with good Saint Nick." I don't know why that song popped in my head as I gather my thoughts to write this chapter. These words are part of the chorus to "Up on the House Top," written by Benjamin Haney in 1864. It's a whimsical Yuletide song that focuses on the fantasy stories of good old Santa Claus.

To read through the lyrics of this song and the story of "'Twas the Night before Christmas" is to allow your thoughts and imaginings to walk through a land of fairy tales where Santa Claus and the imaginary flying reindeer land on your roof, slide down your chimney, and bring gifts for good little girls and boys. These songs and stories move us into a fantastical realm of dreams filled with sugar plum fairies and nutcracker soldiers. They are simply ideas with no basis for reality.

"We have seen incredible things today!" The people cried out to each other that day as they watched a paralytic take up his stretcher, and walk out the door on his own two legs. This was a man who moments before was carried by four friends on the same mat that he now carried. It was described as an incredible, paranormal, and fantastical sight. It was an occurrence that was beyond what their imaginings could possibly stir up. It was a miracle that had never been performed by any Jewish Rabbi.

I present to you the contrast and comparison. Through the centuries we have passed down the fanciful stories of Santa Claus, and with each telling, his personality becomes bigger than life. He's a fat little man that can become small enough to slide down chimneys. We step into the imaginative genre of fiction that involves magic and adventure. We fly to the make believe land of the North Pole.

In contrast, I open up God's Word, His story, and turn to Luke 5:17. The setting was not the imaginary North Pole. It was the real historical life of Palestine in 30 A.D. Jesus was not setting up shop with tiny elves carving wooden toys. He was probably teaching in Simon Peter's home once again. The occurrence was in real time, but what the people exclaimed was the same as our thoughts of Santa Claus. The healing of the paralytic was incredible, unbelievable, and it had never been seen before. So let's begin.

"On one of those days while He was teaching, Pharisees and teachers of the law were sitting there who had come from every village of Galilee and Judea, and also from Jerusalem. *And the Lord's power to heal was in Him*" Luke 5:17 HCSB.

Mark 2 sets the stage for this encounter. "When He entered Capernaum again after some days it was reported that He was at home" Mark 2:1 HCSB. Matthew 9:1 from HCSB gives us the how. "So He got into a boat, crossed over, and came to His own town."

Jesus had recently called Simon Peter, James, John and Andrew to become fishers of men. The four walked away from their business, and left everything to follow Jesus. The group left the Capernaum area and went into all of Galilee. Jesus was preaching in synagogues and driving out demons and healing all kinds of infirmities. His popularity grew and His fame spread all over Palestine. The end result was Jesus could no longer enter a town quietly trying to flying under the radar. People came to Him from everywhere.

Now, Jesus gets into a boat and sails back across the Sea of Galilee and He goes home. He returns to Capernaum where He called the first of His disciples. Jesus was the man of the hour and all the rage. Even the Jewish hierarchy came to check Him out. Pharisees and scribes from every village of Galilee, Judea, and even Jerusalem sat in the house listening to Jesus' teachings. These men considered themselves the guardians of Jewish traditions and laws. Each felt it was his duty to observe this new Rabbi and to check into the validity of Jesus' teachings and miracles. There they sat watching and observing, all the while the healing power of God pulsed through Jesus. It was a power they would never feel nor partake in.

Jesus taught in their midst with the electricity of healing surging through His entire being and there they sat without an ounce of healing power amongst any of them.

Jesus was now so popular the Jewish leaders couldn't ignore Him. The name Pharisee means separated ones. They numbered around 6000. They were the self-appointed guardians of Mosaic Law and Jewish traditions. Jesus threatened their authority and crushed their pride. Thus began the conflict between Jesus and the Jewish religious rulers. It would only escalate from here. He was about to forgive someone's sin and they couldn't tolerate that. It would be labeled blasphemy, for only God could remove a person's wrong doings.

"Just then some men came, carrying on a mat a man who was paralyzed. They tried to bring him in and set him down before Jesus. Since they could not find a way to bring him in because of the crowd, they went up on the roof and lowered him on the mat through the roof tiles into the middle of the crowd before Jesus. Seeing their faith He said, "Friend, your sins are forgiven you." Then the scribes and the Pharisees began to think: "Who is this man who speaks blasphemies? Who can forgive sins but God alone?" Luke 5:18-21 HCSB.

The gauntlet had been thrown down. Jesus had just challenged their belief system. The friction between the Jewish hierarchy and the Son of Man was beginning to ignite sparks. Jesus aggravated them with His declaration that He forgave this man's sins. They claimed only God had that prerogative, but Jesus would prove it was one of His privileges as Son of God.

Jesus came to show the world the nature of God the Father. He arrived on this earth having the heart of God, and that faith moves the heart of God to action.

Four friends, we are never given their names, but they had faith that would move a mountain or at least tiles from the roof. It was a bold move and was probably illegal. I know I would be dialing 911 if someone tried to enter my residence by ripping open my roof, but this was their plan. In their estimation, it was the only way, so they persevered, did the unexpected, and got their friend the audience he needed. The faith of these four friends got Jesus' attention.

While the man lying on a mat received forgiveness, the Pharisees and scribes who stood with arms crossed, received a scathing rebuke from Jesus.

"But perceiving their thoughts, Jesus replied to them, "Why are you thinking this in your hearts? Which is easier; to say, 'Your sins are forgiven you,' or to say 'Get up and walk'? but so you may know that the Son of Man has authority on earth to forgive sins" – He told the paralyzed man, "I tell you: Get up, pick up your mat, and go home" Luke 5:22-24 HCSB.

The faith of the friends animated Jesus to action, but it was the condition of the man on the mat that touched His heart. Every act of healing Jesus performed was unique to that individual. In this instance some sin, some wrong that this man committed in his past had paralyzed him. Jesus saw through the bones, muscle, and tissue, and like an X-Ray technician, He knew the truth and He removed the guilt. "Stand up, take your mat, and go home." The man did just that.

"At once the man stood up before them, picked up his mat and went home, praising God" Luke 5:25 NCV.

Three commands were all that were needed. Enough said. When the man picked up his mat, Jesus' power to forgive sins was proven. The Pharisees and the Scribes shut their mouths for the moment. It was a graphic way to prove Jesus had been given the authority to forgive sins. He is the Son of God after all.

"All the people were fully amazed and began to praise God. They were filled with much respect and said, "Today we have seen amazing things!" Luke 5:25 NCV.

"All the people..." This means everyone including the scribes and Pharisees had their minds blown away in that moment. Jesus had just performed a supernatural feat. It displayed His own prerogative to remove guilt and pay the penalty for sin. Jesus had the power to nullify wrong and assign right standing to this man. This day He removed the physical consequences of this man's guilt. It was visible affirmation of Jesus' intangible power to forgive.

We all miss the mark of God's holiness the same as the paralytic in Luke 5. These stories we find in the Word of God are not whimsical songs of enchanting folklore. Their settings are not somewhere over the rainbow places. They were historic moments set in Palestine in 30 A.D. As the people watched the paralytic rise up and carry his mat out the door to his home, the people declared they had seen a strange thing. It was something the scribes and Pharisees had never nor could ever perform.

Jesus penetrated our ordinary to show us God's extraordinary; taking us into His glorious realm.

Jesus is the same yesterday, today, and tomorrow. God still sees the truth of our paralysis and brokenness. Be encouraged because He still commands us to rise up, carry our mats, and carry everything that keeps us from walking into God's glorious plans for our life. He calls us to take dominion over our deliverance. In other words, "Own His forgiveness and healing in our lives." These stories are true and trustworthy.

The Rooftop

Lutko lay plastered to the stretcher. The pungent aroma of rotting fish filled his nostrils. He could hear the tranquil lapping of the waves as they broke across the Sea of Galilee. He could not see them. The clear sky and the wispy clouds that floated above him was his only horizon. It had been that way for years. Guilt and sorrow had mapped out his life all these many days.

Lutko remembered the day well when his world had crumbled around him. He had savagely lashed out at those closest to him, leaving irreparable damage in the wake of his vicious attacks. The bitterness in his soul had poisoned his mind. Lutko knew he had crossed the line. No one not even Adonai could reach down into his darkness and forgive him. In his heart he knew he had become unforgivable. The talons of that guilt slowly crept into his very own limbs. Day by day his muscles atrophied from lack of movement. He had drunk the wine of anger and rage and it had robbed him of life and movement in his body and soul. Days rolled into weeks, weeks into months, then the months became years.

Lutko's life was lived in emptiness on the fishing shores of Capernaum, but just like Job, Adonai had sent friends who had become his brothers. Life that was once empty was now filled with brotherly love. Philo, Killeon, Levi, and Uriah were the type of friends who sat with him in mud puddles. Day after day they would carry him to a new area of Capernaum. He discovered new sights and sounds that brought variety to a life lived on a stretcher.

Today was a different type of day. Lutko felt it as soon as the foursome approached. Each had a conspiratorial look plastered across their countenance. The four friends picked up their familiar corner of his stretcher, and they set out for this new adventure. From the corner of his eye Lutko saw the house bulging with a sea of humanity. He had heard the rumors swirling around the wharf. The new Rabbi was back in town. Jesus of Nazareth had been traveling through Galilee and the tales of his healing and teachings had blown swiftly across the Sea.

Philo, Killeon, Levi, and Uriah began climbing the steps at the side of the house. Their excitement and confidence in the Healer was contagious. Lutko became caught up in their faith. These four friends would risk all for him. Down below this roof stood the only One in all of Palestine who could cure Lutko's condition. As they lowered him through the damaged roof, Lutko hoped he could convey his deep gratitude to them.

Then he heard the words, "Friend, your sins are forgiven," and he looked into eyes that were filled with mercy and compassion. For so long he had felt removed from the love of Adonai, but now with those five words freely spoken, he was again enveloped in the embrace of a love long forgotten.

Lutko had not worshiped in a long time. All the strength he had once lost now flooded into every fiber of his being. Where guilt had robbed him of movement, forgiveness moved him. He was able to jump to his feet, and carry out the mat which had once carried him. Lutko went home glorifying the Great I Am.

Waypoints to your destination:

What was the one thing that set Jesus apart from the Pharisees and scribes that day in Capernaum?

In verse 20, what did Jesus see in the friends before He said, "Friend, your sins are forgiven."

What would you call that type of faith?

Is there anything in your life that keeps you paralyzed from walking in God's purpose for you?

"Lord God, You are the only One who has the power to restore the broken and paralyzed pieces of my life. Thank you for Your forgiveness and help me carry out the things that hold me back from Your abundant life."

The Land of Misfits

Day Thirty Six

"After this, Jesus went out and saw a tax collector named Levi sitting at the tax office, and He said to him, "Follow Me!" So, leaving everything behind, he got up and began to follow Him" Luke 5:27-28 HCSB.

"Hey, Lucas' grandma, I invited Lucas to my birthday party." The six year old with muffled hair informed me. It was at that point each of Lucas' friends chimed in, "Me too, me too!" The party became the talk of the lunch table and Lucas clued me in on what they were going to do at the party. They were friends and buddies and they had fun playing together. It is the definition of a party. It's a social gathering of invited guests, typically involving eating and drinking and entertainment, and Jesus made the guest list of some of the most notorious parties of His day.

In Matthew, chapter 9, Mark, chapter 2, and Luke, chapter 5, we find Jesus in conflict with the religious authorities once again because He deliberately associated with outcasts and sinners. These people did not observe the Law that the Pharisees so ardently guarded. It was outrageous for Jesus to spend time and effort on them. Jesus even called one of the tax collectors to become His disciple. Tax collectors were despised in Israel during that day because of their reputation for corruption. Tax collectors were known to extort more taxes than were required by Roman law.

These funds were then pocketed by the local tax collector. This was where Jesus' path intersected the life of one of these despicable outcasts.

His name is Matthew in the gospel of Matthew chapter 9. Mark and Luke call him by another name, Levi. He was Jewish but working for the enemy. Perhaps he should have pursued a religious calling as a Levite, like his name would suggest, instead Matthew chose a different road. It was a lucrative road. His countrymen saw it as a road to perdition, but Jesus changed that trajectory. When others saw a hated publican, Jesus saw a gift from God that day as He passed by Matthew's tax collector's booth.

"Follow me," was Jesus' invitation as He passed by. It was a simple two word command, but Matthew was touched and honored by the words. They were personal to him. Not many of his fellow neighbors even spoke to him, but here was a Rabbi that went out of His way to invite him in.

The invitation made him feel special. Jesus was asking Matthew to follow Him as a student. He called Matthew to walk a new road. It would be a road of separation and altruism. In this invitation Jesus asked Levi to leave behind his sordid past of fraudulent practices. It was a call to a lifestyle change, leaving behind opulence for poverty. He wouldn't gain material riches walking side by side with Jesus. Matthew was called to burn the bridge of dishonesty and walk with Jesus down a road of righteousness.

The name Matthew means gift of God. That day beside a booth Jesus gave a despised tax collector the gift of acceptance. Kevin and I named our son Matthew, Matthew Landry Jones. Landry and Whitney named their son Matthew, Ezekiel Matthew Jones. Others may not see them as gifts but I see them as I know they are, God's gift to our family.

Apparently, Matthew Levi decided Jesus' calling was higher than his current profitable business because he immediately stood up and followed Jesus. No longer sitting behind a booth collecting tariffs, Levi rose. He put into action all that he was feeling. He left everything behind except his writing quill for one day he would write about the day Jesus called him to become more. Matthew Levi was designed by God for a higher, more honorable calling than to cheat people of hard earned income.

It was an outrageous action for Jesus to call a tax collector, but that was what He came to do. He came to show us scandalous love. His was a love that cast His lot with sinners and outcasts. They were the people who recognized their need for mercy, and He made them feel comfortable in His presence. He made them feel special.

Matthew was so overjoyed at Jesus' invitation, he wanted to honor Jesus with a dinner party. Matthew's guest list included many more notorious, and notable sinners of Capernaum and the surrounding communities. They were the ones who were whispered about behind their backs. They would have been shunned by polite company, but Jesus went and reclined with them at Matthew's banquet table.

"Then Levi hosted a grand banquet for Him at his house. Now there was a large crowd of tax collectors and others who were guests with them" Luke 5:29 HCSB.

Their reputations were soiled to be sure. They were the outcast and disreputable of religious society. The people sitting with Jesus at the table were known to be especially wicked. The religious elite considered this group incorrigible and beyond redemption. These guests often made the party scene and were the rabble edge of polite society. They did not frequent synagogues or keep the Sabbath. Those who were excluded from mainstream religion were invited to this gala. Jesus deliberately associated with the misfits of society. He mixed comfortably with them because He came to seek and save people exactly like them. They were the fringe people.

It was a festive meal. Matthew Levi had the means and the money to make this a grand affair alight with entertainment. His house was in the upper echelon neighborhood. The atmosphere was honest and without pretension. The meal was served at a table low enough for the guest to recline on a mat while leaning on their left elbow. It was intimate table fellowship and was an expression of trust, identity, and a honest desire to seek a new friendship. These guests were interested in Jesus and what He had to share. They felt comfortable in His presence because He sat with them and did not condemn them or preach at them.

He shared a meal and conversation with them. Jesus got to know them before He would call them to change. He asked about their stories. He got acquainted with them. These people were not rejects to Jesus. He invited them into His world. The call to repentance was not at the top of His "to do" list at this soirée. To Jesus, these people were patients who needed a physician. His care and protection of them was authentic and brought out a fierceness in Him.

The Pharisees and scribes had assimilated their own ladder to climb up and approach God, but Jesus was slowly dismantling it one rung at a time. He had just invited defectives, riffraff, and according to their words, scum, to the banqueting table. It turned their stomachs. They were furious at how lax Jesus was to observe their laws.

"But the Pharisees and their scribes were complaining to His disciples, "Why do you eat and drink with tax collectors and sinners?" Jesus replied to them, "The healthy don't need a doctor, but the sick do. I have not come to call the righteous, but sinners to repentance" Luke 5:30-31 HCSB.

Jesus took offense at the Pharisee's presumptive attitude. Jesus' sensitive soul did not coddle up to the scribes and Pharisees. He called them to account for their self-righteousness and hypocrisy. They were quick to diagnose what was wrong with other people, but couldn't see the wretchedness and corruption inside of their own souls. The masks they wore in public eroded the care and compassion they should have held for the people they were supposed to serve. They appeared clean on the outside which made the people hold them in high esteem.

They were zealous guardians of the law and their zeal made them callous to the people's needs. In this scene they literally pitched a tizzy fit. They lit into the disciples when they saw Jesus eating with publicans and sinners. The NLT says in Luke 5:30, "Why do you eat and drink with such scum?"

Jesus called the Pharisees and scribes to account and did not let them slander this group of outcasts. The Pharisees could not see the dirt and grime inside themselves because they only had eyes to see the filth of the world. It was a difference of depth perception. Jesus saw the sickness that crippled society and the Pharisees saw the sick society that threatened their way of life.

Asher, my oldest grandson, was telling me about the birthday party he had been invited to. "La, (that is what he calls me these days), we are going to play lacrosse till 9 pm." Asher felt special to be invited to this party. This group was his peeps. He wanted to hang out with them. They had things in common. Asher and his friends were going to hang out, relax and just be boys. They were comfortable in each other's presence.

That's the party to which Jesus invites us. Come and be who you are. Take off your mask. He loves and accepts you. He hates pretension. His invitation is a special calling because you are precious in His eyes. Your past and your present cannot exclude you from His guest list. There is no depth that is too deep that Jesus' forgiveness cannot reach.

Two thousand years ago Jesus came to make a house call. The people He had created were ill and needed a physician. We are the same people. Sin and shame has caused tumors in our souls. Jesus came to seek and to save those who recognize their need for forgiveness and healing.

Jesus opened up a new avenue to the Father. That day the Pharisees were on the outside looking in. Don't be the one with crossed arms looking down on the dregs of society. Jesus invites you into the banqueting table. The only requirement for admittance: acknowledge that you are sin sick and need Jesus' forgiveness.

There is room for you to recline at the table next to Jesus and tell Him your story. He will make you feel welcome. His Presence will envelop you. You will also hear Him say, "Come follow me."

Party Time

Matthew sat at the booth watching the fishing vessel offloading its fresh catch. Their nets were full. The night's haul had been prosperous for this fleet of fisherman. He breathed in a ragged sigh as he toggled with the hidden weights of the scale. Roman coin would line his pockets at the end of this day. He could feel the weight of the gold even now, just as he felt the emptiness of his life.

Riches and opulence had become like a brick around his neck. Friends and neighbors came and went just as quickly. His life was void of any real relationships. Walking home every night in the dark just reflected the darkness of his soul. He was lonely. His friends were really just acquaintances who were as superficial as he was.

Matthew's business was located on the Great West Road that followed from Damascus to the Mediterranean Sea. It was a lucrative and profitable tariff office because of its location. It had also become a burden in his life because his countrymen held him in contempt. Matthew had even cheated family members through the years. Money was his only companion.

Matthew watched as the Pharisees and scribes passed his office. He laughed derisively as they walked across the road to avoid contaminating the soles of their sandals with dust from his business.

That's when He saw the Rabbi, Jesus of Nazareth. Matthew noticed Jesus did not cross the road to avoid him. Jesus was heading straight for his booth and there was a broad, authentic smile that began to spread across the Rabbi's face. The grin was genuine and brought a twinkle into Jesus' eyes.

Matthew assumed Jesus was greeting someone behind so he turned. There was no one. The smile and the greeting were meant for him. It had been quite some time since any one of his countrymen had greeted him so warmly or even acknowledged his existence at all.

The Rabbi wrapped him in an embrace. Matthew heard the words, "Follow me," spoken from those hallowed lips. In that moment the void of nothingness in Matthew's soul was filled. The gold bars that felt like shackles became nothing to him. He had been included. Where others saw worthlessness, with those words spoken Jesus had made him feel worthy. Matthew knew this feeling that had been absent from his life for so long was exactly what he needed to feel purposeful again. He didn't need Roman coin to give him validity, Matthew needed to be included and Jesus made him feel special. He rose and closed up shop. He had a party to prepare.

Waypoints to your destination:

What do you think Matthew's life was like as a tax collector?

Do you think he ever felt he had done things that were beyond redemption?

What does his name mean?

What is the difference that Jesus saw between the guests at the party and the Pharisees?

Is there any action that is beyond Jesus' forgiveness?

"Lord, thank you for including even me. I thank you there is nothing beyond Your redemption. God, I recognize my need of Your forgiveness. Thank you for saving my soul."

Where in the World Did They Go?

Day Thirty Seven

"At that time Jesus went off to a mountain to pray, and He spent the night praying to God. The next morning, Jesus called His followers to Him and chose twelve of them, whom He named apostles: Simon (Jesus named him Peter), his brother Andrew, James, John, Philip, Bartholomew, Matthew, Thomas, James son of Alphaeus, Simon (called the Zealot), Judas son of James, and Judas Iscariot, who later turned Jesus over to His enemies" Luke 6:12-16 NCV.

"Where's Waldo?" My children loved seeking out the hidden Waldos in pictures, puzzles, and books. While writing this book, I have begun to wonder, "Where's the disciples?" What happened to them?

"Once upon a time..." Jesus called out twelve men and with these twelve He wrote a story of healing and redemption. These twelve weren't pillars of Jewish religion nor were they professional clergymen. Not one of them ever studied under a revered rabbi. They lived ordinary lives in Palestine under Roman rule in 30 A.D. On the day Jesus called them out to become His ambassadors, their ordinary lives became extraordinary. Jesus wrote a one-of-a-kind story with their lives. It was a story that began a movement that has lasted two thousand years. Jesus didn't choose these men because of their eloquence or charismatic personality. Often they displayed characteristics of impatience, greed, anger, and pride, but still Jesus called them.

Jesus chose them after a full night of talking with His Father in heaven. It was in spite of their faults that He called them out to become His representatives. In essence, their personalities were our personalities, and it gives us courage to see our story written out in their stories. We relate to their everyday lives. These twelve weren't the most interesting men in the world before Jesus intersected their lives. That is why we see ourselves in them. Let's take a closer look. Who do you most relate to?

Simon was the first that Jesus nicknamed. "And I tell you that you are Peter, and on this rock I will build my church, and the gates of Hades will not overpower it" Matthew 16:18 NET. He was impetuous by nature being the first to confess Jesus as the Christ, the Son of the living God and the first to deny Jesus at His trial. Peter was also the first to run head long into the empty grave.

He had the gift of gab, and talked when he should have been reverent. "Peter said to Jesus, 'Lord it is good for us to be here. If you want, I will make three shelters – one for You, one for Moses, and one for Elijah.' While he was still speaking, a bright cloud overshadowed them and a voice from the cloud said, "This is my one dear Son, in whom I take great delight. Listen to Him!" Matthew 17:4-5 NET. He was braggadocios. "But Peter insisted emphatically, 'Even if I must die with You, I will never deny You.' And all of them said the same thing" Mark 14:31 NET.

During the first years of the early church, even then, Peter had his faults and the apostle Paul called him out on them. "When Peter came to Antioch, I challenged him to his face because he was wrong" Galatians 2:11 NCV.

In spite of Peter's faults and boasts, before Jesus ascended to heaven, His last challenge to Peter, "Feed My lambs," "Take care of My sheep," "Feed My sheep" John 21 NCV. Peter was the mouthpiece and the head of the apostles on the day of Pentecost according to Acts chapter two. His letters in 1st and 2nd Peter proclaim the doctrine of our salvation and warnings against false teachings.

Peter loved the Lord Jesus Christ, "Lord, You know everything; You know that I love You" John 21:17 NCV. In the end Peter suffered much for proclaiming the name of Jesus. Sometime in 60 A.D., during the persecution of the church under Emperor Nero, Peter was executed for his belief in Jesus Christ.

Andrew, the second disciple on this list, had his own personality quirks. He was very inquisitive and was not afraid to take his inquiries to Jesus. "Another of his followers, Andrew, Simon Peter's brother, said, "Here is a boy with five loaves of barley bread and two little fish, but that is not enough for so many people" John 6:8 NCV. Jesus would then take that small meal and feed five thousand.

Andrew was often associated amongst Jesus' inner circle. "Later, as Jesus was sitting on the Mount of Olives, opposite the Temple, he was alone with Peter, James, John, and Andrew. They asked Jesus, "Tell us, when will these things happen? And what will be the sign that they are going to happen?" Mark 13:3-4 NCV.

Andrew was the first missionary. He brought Simon Peter to meet Jesus. Christians in what is now the Soviet Union claim Andrew as the first to bring the gospel to their land. History indicates Andrew also preached in Asia Minor, modern-day Turkey, and in Greece, where he is believed to have been martyred there.

James and John were brothers and sons of Zebedee. They were Galilean fishermen when Jesus met them. Jesus nicknamed them, "Sons of Thunder," most likely for the zeal they displayed for Jesus' honor. "When James and John, followers of Jesus, saw this, they said, "Lord, do you want us to call fire down from heaven and destroy those people?" Luke 9:54 NCV.

These two also caused strife among The Twelve. Their mom came and asked Jesus a special request, "Then the wife of Zebedee came to Jesus with her sons. She bowed before Him and asked Him to do something for her. Jesus asked, 'What do you want?' She said, "Promise that one of my sons will sit at your right side and the other will sit at your left side in your kingdom" Matthew 20:20-21 NCV. Despite all that, both were part of Jesus' inner circle.

John was so keenly aware of the love Jesus bore for him that he called himself the "beloved." He became the leader of the church in the Ephesus area. As Jesus hung on the cross, He asked John to take care of His mother. During Domitian's persecution of Christians in the middle of the 90's, John was exiled to the island of Patmos. At Patmos John received the revelation of Jesus and there he wrote the last book of the Bible.

James was beheaded by Herod Agrippa 1 in the year 44 A.D. "During that same time King Herod began to mistreat some who belonged to the church. He ordered James, the brother of John, to be killed by the sword" Acts 12:1-2 NCV.

Philip had his own set of questions. He asked Jesus for a vision of the Father, "Philip said to Him, 'Lord show us the Father. That is all we need" John 14:8 NCV. Jesus would tell

Philip that he had already seen the Father in Himself. Philip acted as an intermediary between Jesus and the Greeks who wanted to be introduced to Jesus according to John 12. Philip brought his friend Nathanael to Jesus. According to "Fox's Book of Martyrs," Philip went to North Africa and then into Asia Minor. He converted the wife of a Roman proconsul who then had Philip arrested and brutally put to death.

Bartholomew was most likely the Nathanael that Philip brought to Jesus in John chapter 1. "But Nathanael said to Philip, 'Can anything good come from Nazareth?' Philip answered, 'Come and see.' As Jesus saw Nathanael coming toward him, He said, 'Here is truly an Israelite. There is nothing false in him" John 1:46-47 NCV. Tradition attributes that Bartholomew went with Thomas on mission trips to India, Armenia, Ethiopia, and Southern Arabia. A document called the "Martyrdom of Bartholomew," states, "And when he had thus spoken, the king was informed that this god Baldad and all the other idols had fallen down, and were broken in pieces. Then the king rent the purple in which he was clothed and ordered the holy apostle Bartholomew to be beaten with rods; and after having been thus scourged to be beheaded."

Matthew was the notorious tax collector and writer of the gospel of Matthew. He was said to have spread the gospel in Persia and Ethiopia. Again, according to "Fox's Book of Martyrs," Matthew was executed with a spear.

Thomas was called the doubter. "But Thomas said, 'I will not believe it until I see the nail marks in His hands and put my finger where the nails were and put my hand into His side." Tradition has Thomas preaching in Syria and India. "Thomas, called Didymus, preached the Gospel in Parthia and India, where he excited the rage of the pagan priests, he was martyred by being thrust through with a spear," states "Fox's Book of Martyrs."

James the son of Alphaeus, could have been the brother of Matthew who was also the son of Alphaeus, "While Jesus was walking along, He saw a man named Levi (Matthew) son of Alphaeus, sitting in the tax collector's booth" Mark 2:14 NCV. The historian, Josephus, reported that James was stoned, then clubbed to death.

Simon called the zealot was a Jewish loyalist and political nationalist before coming to follow Jesus. "Fox's Book of Martyrs," says of him, "Surnamed Zelotes, preached the Gospel in Mauritania, Africa, and even in Britain, in which latter country he was crucified, A.D. 74." The story goes he was killed after refusing to sacrifice to the sun god.

Judas not Judas Iscariot, but the son of James, lacked understanding. "Then Judas (not Judas Iscariot) said, "But, Lord, why do you plan to show yourself to us and not to the rest of the world?" John 14:22 NCV. He didn't understand how the kingdom of God was to come unless the Messiah made His public disclosure.

Then we come to the betrayer, Judas Iscariot, who turned Jesus over to His enemies. He betrayed Jesus with a kiss. Judas then killed himself. "So Judas threw the money into the temple and left. Then he went away and hanged himself" Matthew 27:5 NIV. He was the treasurer of the group and was offended when Mary poured perfume on Jesus' feet and wiped His feet with her hair. "But one of his disciples, Judas Iscariot, who was later to betray him objected, 'Why wasn't this perfume sold and the money given to the poor? It was worth a year's wages'" John 12:4-5 NIV. He also opened a door into his life for Satan to enter. "Satan entered Judas Iscariot, one of Jesus' twelve apostles" Luke 22:3 NCV.

Their stories aren't pretty. From our vantage point they did not get their "happily ever after" ending. God, however, knows the rest of the story. For eleven of them, they are part of the twenty-four elders in Revelation 4:10 NCV, "Then the twenty-four elders bow down before the One who sits on the throne and they worship Him who lives forever and ever. They put their crowns down before the throne and say: 'You are worthy, our Lord and God, to receive glory and honor and power, because You made all things. Everything existed and was made, because You wanted it."

The Twelve were a kaleidoscope of personalities and were as varied as the threads of a royal tapestry. Eleven of those first twelve would go out into all parts of the known world at that time to spread the good news that Jesus saves. Each of their stories were just part of a whole story, His Story, but when woven together we see our reflection in each of them.

Stories are passed down from one generation to another. They are the primary way generations pass history and truth to the children of the next generation. Stories captivate us. I miss hearing my dad tell stories of gathering water in barrels from his neighbor's well, or that his mother sewed his shirts from flour sacks.

God wired us to love stories. My grandson, Asher, loves to regale us with stories from history lessons. He knows the most unusual facts about Albert Einstein. It is part of our DNA to love stories because we are created by the greatest Storyteller.

We think our stories have to be interesting to make them relevant to our culture, but since God is the One writing them, it is God who will add all the twists and climaxes onto the blank pages of our lives. He is writing a story that is relatable to a hurting world. Someone out there needs to hear our story. They need a Hero and we aren't it. The main character of our story is Jesus. The main character of their stories was Jesus.

The Nighttime Prayer

Jesus left the encampment in the dark stillness of the nighttime sky. He left behind the stress of the day that was spent arguing with the Pharisees, and teaching the sea of people pressing into Him for wisdom and healing. He was spent, but He knew His source of energy came from spending time with His Father. While everyone bedded down for the night, Jesus sought strength in communion with the One who had sent Him.

He did not begin with, "Now I lay me down to sleep..." No, He was one with the Father. They shared the same passion and desires. He had helped the Father create these people. Theirs was a relationship built on oneness with each other. Their conversations were intimate. "Father, who is in heaven," Jesus began to speak while the Father leaned in to listen.

From Jesus' mouth to the Father's ear, the two sat together in earnest conversation. They had a plan. It was unfolding as they spoke to each other. Jesus asked, "Whom shall I send?" The Father spoke their names one by one. Each knew there was one on the list who had a darkness in his soul, yet still the Father spoke his name, "Judas Iscariot."

One hour passed, then a second, to them it felt like no time until the sun was rising in the east. Jesus was exhilarated after spending this night with the Father whom He loved above all things. The individual names of the tribe of ambassadors that He would summon on this day were engraved on His palm. He would send them out with His authority. They would make mistakes for sure, but eleven of these men would spread His good news into every part of the world.

Waypoints to your destination:

Who do you most relate to on this list?

What is the personality trait that reminds you of yourself?

Do you ever feel like you're not good enough to be Jesus' representative in this world?

How do their stories encourage you?

"God, I'm just me, ordinary me. My testimony isn't heart stopping or tear dropping, but it is mine. You are writing it. You said we will triumph over Your enemy by the blood of the Lamb and the word of our testimony. Thank you for their stories. Thank you that You don't choose perfect people to tell Your Story, but that You perfect the people You choose."

The Schoolyard

Day Thirty Eight

"Now when Jesus saw the crowds, He went up on a mountainside and sat down. His disciples came to Him and He began to teach them" Matthew 5:1-2a NIV.

I always love the excitement of starting a new school year. I loved it as a child. I loved it when my kids were school age, and now, I love watching my grandsons prepare for a new school year. A new chapter is about to be written into the story of their young lives as they begin each new grade. New skills will be introduced. My grandson, Lucas, will begin first grade this fall. He will start spelling tests and reading full books. Asher will start fifth grade, and whole new levels of math will be introduced. New friendships will be made and old friendships will be resumed.

As a little girl, I loved picking out new notebooks while vowing to be really organized this year if I could just have the special notebook with all the secret pockets. And who didn't love choosing that special lunchbox with all the new cartoon characters that would be introduced into the Saturday morning fall lineup. Can't you feel the anticipation building as you remember going to school to check out which teacher you got and what friends you had in your class that year. "School days, school days, dear old golden rule days." In Matthew chapter 5 Jesus had gathered His students and the school bell had been rung. The Twelve had been called in from the school yard and now the real teaching would begin. They were about to learn a new path and a different perspective on the Law.

It was the Sermon on the Mount and it set Jesus' teachings apart from all other Torah schools of His day. It is known as the greatest sermon ever given. The depth and magnitude of His words came because the Orator lived their meaning. Jesus began teaching the Twelve how to see people and view the world as He did. His teachings weren't written out on chalkboard or paper; they were written in the way He lived His life. We call them the Beatitudes and you will be blessed if you follow them.

Like Rocky Balboa leading his fans up the 72 stone steps to the Philadelphia Museum of art, like Forrest Gump running across America with hundreds joining the trail, so Jesus led the masses through the shores and mountains of Galilee. With each new healing and miracle more were added to the great throng of people who pressed in to hear, see, and touch the Rabbi from Galilee. They were ordinary people, blue collar workers just trying to survive in this world ruled by Rome.

There is a plaque mounted inside the pedestal of the Statue of Liberty. It is a poem written in the 1900s by Emma Lazarus. A line of the poem reads, "Give me your tired, your poor, your huddled masses yearning to breathe free." These were the types of people who followed Jesus outside of Capernaum this day. The disciples did not see what our Savior saw as He climbed the mountainside to deliver His Sermon. They could not. They had not yet been given Jesus' perception of human life and its worth. On this day He gave them their first Social Study lesson.

Like most teachers of the day, Jesus taught from a seated position and when their revered teacher sat, then the disciples gathered round Him to listen. With the masses spread before Him, Jesus began. He opened His mouth and used the tired, the hungry and the poor as His object lesson.

In a world where everyone was searching for their zen or their happy place, in a world that felt like its axis was constantly on tilt, Jesus taught how to find balance and that inner peace. The words He spoke two thousand years ago rang true then, and they ring true today because the stress and turmoil in the world does not change.

"Blessed are..." In the 70's and 80's Calgon bath soap released a commercial series with the tag line, "Calgon take me away." The inference being, soaking in a Calgon bath can take away the stress of the day. When Jesus spoke the Beatitudes, He was giving a different formula for a Shangri-La type of day. Inward peace comes to us when we follow His precepts.

True happiness that is produced at the core level of our souls comes from experiencing favor with God. Happiness begins when we recognize our great need to be forgiven, we are devoid of spiritual arrogance. We must see ourselves as we are: people who have done wrong and cannot work their way into God's good graces. In our spiritual poverty we reach out for God's forgiveness and He refreshes us. His Kingdom in which all things are consummately perfect becomes ours for the taking. In this first Beatitude Jesus says, "For theirs **is** the Kingdom of heaven." "Is," it's a current verb meaning now, meaning forever. Those who realize they are lost without Jesus have an inexhaustible inheritance with God that begins now.

Dear reader and friend, Do you know Him today? Don't you want this inner peace that Jesus spoke of. "Blessed are the poor in spirit, for theirs is the kingdom of heaven" Matthew 5:3 NIV.

"Blessed are those who mourn, for they will be comforted" Matthew 5:4 NIV. This is a grief that is too great to bear. It is manifested grief that takes possession of a person and it cannot be hidden from others. Dear reader, have you been there? Has life taken you to your knees in great sadness? I have. I have heard myself cry out, "Why?" And "When will this end?" Jesus promises comfort will come to those in this condition. When we mourn and lament over all the wrongs we have done, Jesus promises to come and lift the burden of our guilt. Comfort, it is a welcoming hand extended to someone who is bereft. Jesus comes along right beside us and takes our sorrow upon Himself. Dear reader, give Him your mourning.

"Blessed are the meek for they will inherit the earth" Matthew 5:5 NIV. Mild, gentle, long-suffering, and patient, these traits seem to be absent today in a world where everything is at our fingertips. I shut my computer down within a minute if it does not instantly load the internet. I reboot the modem within two minutes if it does not respond to my page request. We have become a society that demands instant access. Long-suffering and patience are on the back burner, but Jesus promises an inheritance if we will be gentle with our reactions when our coffee is sloshed out, when our life gets bumped, or when our toe is stumped. The humble and gentle will inherit the earth. This earth is simply God's theatre. Each scene in our life becomes eternally significant. God is just waiting to reward our gentle answers.

"Blessed are those who hunger and thirst for righteousness for they will be filled" Matthew 5:6 NIV. I'm hungry right now. I desire food. This makes me reflect on these words. I will find contentment when I actively seek right standing with God. Am I, are you? Do we earnestly desire to be right with God? Jesus promises that we will be satisfied and filled the moment we come seeking Him. Dear reader, have you taken time to seek God today?

"Blessed are the merciful, for they will be shown mercy" Matthew 5:7 NIV. The compassionate will receive compassion from God. "Then the King will say to those on His right, 'Come you who are blessed by my Father take your inheritance, the kingdom prepared for you since the creation of the world. For I was hungry and you gave Me something to eat, I was thirsty and you gave Me something to drink, I was a stranger and you invited me in," Matthew 25:34-35 NIV.

"Blessed are the pure in heart for they will see God" Matthew 5:8 NIV. Oh to recognize God with us, to see Him as you sit, to know His nearness as you rise, and to feel His presence as you go through your day. Jesus promises that we will see God when our heart is pure. To be pure is to be uncontaminated by our world. Our thoughts are to be unmixed with the undesirable elements this world produces. The only way to reach this state is for Jesus to purge our lives from the things we have allowed to contaminate us. Then, that thin veil between heaven and earth will be lifted and we can see God as Isaiah did. "In the year that King Uzziah died, I saw the Lord, high and exalted, seated on a throne; and the train of His robe filled the temple" Isaiah 6:1 NIV.

"Blessed are the peacemakers for they will be called children of God" Matthew 5:9 NIV. Peacemakers are different from peacekeepers. In God's kingdom a peacemaker is someone who bravely declares God's terms which make people whole. We are incomplete without Jesus. Some may not like that declaration. Some may accuse me of being politically biased by stating that fact, but because Jesus has called me to speak the truth in love, I must stay true to my beliefs. You need Jesus. I need Jesus. The world needs Jesus for without Him chaos reigns. "For you are all sons of God through faith in Christ Jesus" Galatians 3:26 HCSB.

I sat at the lake this weekend enjoying the quiet peace the ripples of water made as they washed up on the shore. The hills that surround Lake Tenkiller reminded me of the mountain Jesus might have climbed the morning He spoke the Sermon on the Mount. The Beatitudes floated into my thoughts. "Blessed are..." My grandsons broke into my reverie. They played a spirited game of "King of the Lilly Pad." Who could throw the other brother off the floating pad? The game stood in stark contrast to Jesus' sermon I had just been contemplating. I wonder if Jesus' listeners noticed the same difference. Many of His disciples were expecting military might and power from their long awaited Messiah, yet Jesus taught everything but that. His sermon was laced with calls to humility, meekness, gentleness, peacemaking and perseverance in persecution.

It was Social Studies 101. Jesus the Great Teacher observed the schoolyard before Him. Many of His followers were playing their own version of "King of the Hill." Most were grinding away trying to stay ahead of the next person. Jesus sat down, rang the school bell, and taught a different set of precepts for His students. His teachings were revolutionary. They were a way of peace and wholeness when others called for government overthrow.

When the disciples looked out at the masses and saw only the poor and needy. Jesus saw their true condition and He had compassion on them. He laid out a plan where they can find true inner happiness no matter the circumstances. His words laid a path to contentment two thousand years ago and they still lead us to our Calgon type of day. He moved mountains to reveal the passage way to green pastures and still waters.

The Zealot

Simon sat down among The Twelve. They had followed their Master and Teacher up the mountainside. Classes were about to begin. Every Rabbi had his own Torah school. Simon felt special to be a part of this classroom. Jesus had called him specifically.

Simon was aggravated this day. He had passed a Roman guard as he snaked his way through the countryside following Jesus. By nature he wanted to stir up trouble for this guard, but he held his tongue. Surely Jesus was about to lay out a plan to rid Israel of Roman rule. He ground his teeth as he sat. Why did he always seem to be seated next to Matthew the tax collector? They were natural enemies. One worked for Rome and the other worked to overthrow Rome.

Simon heard Jesus' words, "Blessed are the peacemakers for they will be called sons of God." His churning, agitated spirit began to quiet with each new, "Blessed are..." and he couldn't figure out why. It seemed the words of Jesus had a power all their own to create an inner calmness that the Zealot had been unable to obtain for all these years.

On the Way

Waypoints to your destination:

What do you think "poor in spirit" means?

What happens when you hunger and thirst after God?

What is the difference between Jesus' teachings and how the world teaches us?

How can you obtain that inner peace and wholeness?

"Dear Lord, I want to be at peace with You. I long for wholeness and balance with You. Lord I come hungering and thirsting after You. Fill me this day with Your Presence."

Moving On

Day Thirty Nine

"When He had concluded all His sayings in the hearing of the people, He entered Capernaum" Luke 7:1 HCSB.

"When He entered Capernaum, a centurion came to Him, pleading with Him, 'Lord, my servant is lying at home paralyzed, in terrible agony!'" Matthew 8:5-6 HCSB.

"Jesus marveled at this. He turned around and said to the crowd who had followed Him, 'Listen, everyone! Never had I found even one among the people of God a man like this who believes so strongly in me.' Jesus then spoke the healing word from a distance" Luke 7:9-10 Passion Translation.

"When the Lord saw her, He had compassion on her and said, "Don't cry." Then He came up and touched the open coffin, and the pallbearer stopped. And He said, "Young man, I tell you get up!" Luke 7:13-14 HCSB.

Two grieving parents whose lives intersected Jesus' as He traveled on the way to the cross. Two differing stories that moved Him to take action. One was a Roman, a Gentile, and an outsider, yet still Jesus was moved to act. The other was a widow who lost her only son. She never asked Jesus for help, yet His compassion compelled Him to reach out and give it.

Grieving parents, we find them in doctor's offices and hospitals. There is a disease out there that brings devastation, and it sweeps through families. A broad term for it is "pediatric cancer." Even as I write these two words there is a pit in my stomach and tears are forming in my eyes. Panic is threatening to choke my larynx. The disease has not touched my family, but it has entered my world. One of my daughter's best friends heard the word, "Leukemia," spoken over her six year old daughter. A few years before that, one of my friend's two year old granddaughter was diagnosed with neuroblastoma.

The disease disrupted their worlds. Each family has been changed and marked by these terrible cancers. Two innocent little girls have spent days, weeks, and months in agony. They have battled, they have shown their strength and both have come out on top. God is their victor and Jesus their hero. Today I dedicate this chapter to Hollace Costello, her mom Amy, her dad Brendan, and her sister Langley. I give a shout out to Charlotte York and her family. You guys are heroes in my book and rockstars with powerful stories to tell because of all you have been through and will go through still. You've got this, but more importantly God's got this I have seen each of you grow stronger since the days you first heard the diagnosis. What was sent to destroy, God used to grow a mighty faith.

Jesus has seen your sorrow and He was moved. It was the same emotion that stirred Him when He met the centurion and the widow of Nain. They loved their children the same as you love yours. The Passion Version says in verse 2 of Luke chapter seven, "There He found a Roman military captain who had a beloved servant he valued highly, and the servant was sick to the point of death." In verse 13 of the Passion Bible, "When the Lord saw the grieving mother His heart broke for her. With great tenderness He said to her, "Please don't cry.""

The same heart that broke over the widow's state of affairs, still breaks today. Jesus heard your cries every time

Hollace and Charlotte were hooked up to another IV, and He felt their pain as the medicine that was meant to heal, tore through them, and tormented them as much as the disease that threatened their very lives.

The day my daughter got the news of Hollace's leukemia, she called me, "Mom, would you please pray for Hollace, and Amy, and Brendan, and Langley?" Then she put it on Facebook and called all prayer warriors. "The centurion heard of Jesus and sent some elders of the Jews to Him asking Him to come and heal His servant" Luke 7:3 NIV. When our world gets rocked, we need people to help us. We need intercessors. The centurion needed them and the Costello's needed them.

The Jewish elders went to Jesus with great emotion. "When they came to Jesus, they pleaded earnestly with Him, "This man deserves to have You do this, because he loves our nation and has built our synagogue. So Jesus went with them" Luke 7:4-6 NIV. Emotion, the word comes from the Latin word, "emovere," meaning to move out. The elder's pleas caused Jesus to move toward someone who was outside the Jewish faith. The day Nikki called asking for prayer, I heard the emotion in her voice because she was heartbroken for her friend. I was immediately choked up also. I could feel the groans of my prayers rising toward heaven's throne room.

"In the same way, the Spirit helps us in our weakness. We do not know what we ought to pray for, but the Spirit himself intercedes for us through wordless groans" Romans 8:26 NIV.

"So Jesus went with them. He was not far from the house when the centurion sent friends to say to Him: 'Lord, don't trouble yourself, for I do not deserve to have You come under my roof'" Luke 7:6 NIV.

"Blessed are the poor in spirit for theirs is the kingdom of heaven" Matthew 5:3 NIV. Romans were not known for their humility, yet the Roman centurion recognized his unworthiness before the Great Physician. As each of Hollace's prayer warriors interceded before God, we approached His throne of grace recognizing our great need of a Savior and a Healer.

Jesus marveled at this man's faith. "Jesus then spoke the healing word from a distance" Luke 7:10 Passion Bible. "Mom," Nikki called. There was exuberance in her tone. "Hollace is in remission."

The widow's story was the same. In the end she sang a victor's song, though she never requested Jesus' help. Nain was about twenty-five miles from Capernaum. Jesus met a funeral procession as He entered. For the widow of Nain this was the end of all things, but for Jesus, this was just the middle of her story. The climax was yet to come.

The mourning and the wails of this entourage stood in stark contrast to the jubilant echoes of the crowd that followed Jesus. Death met Him at the entrance of this village, but life would wave good-bye. A cold dead body carried on a wicker stretcher blocked His path to the village. The woman dressed in black at the back of the procession was the dead boy's mother, and it wasn't her first time to don the black outfit. The Bible says she was a widow. At some point in her life she had buried her husband, but during that processional she had a son's hand to hold onto. Now, she would have no companionship when she went home to an empty house that night.

Her story was about to continue though. "When the Lord saw her, His heart overflowed with compassion. "Don't cry!" He said. Then He walked over to the coffin and touched it, and the bearers stopped. "Young man," He said, "I tell you, get up."

Then the dead boy sat up and began to talk! And Jesus gave him back to his mother" Luke 7:13-15 NIV. Enough said.

Sorrow, faith, humility, and emotion. God sees it all, and it is His compassion that moves Him to act on behalf of His creation. The Greek word for compassion means, "to be moved in the inward parts." The Latin word means, "to suffer with."

That was how Jesus felt when He met the centurion and the widow. That was what He felt when He heard the prayers rise up for Hollace and Charlotte. God saw the tears of Hollace's and Charlotte's parents as they checked their children into the hospital. He felt their pain and He suffered with them as they heard the diagnosis, "cancer." That was what He felt then and it is what He feels now. The same Jesus who entered the centurion's and the widow's story is the same Jesus who enters our stories.

"Who shall separate us from the love of Christ? Shall trouble or hardship or persecution or famine or nakedness or danger or sword? As it is written: "For your sake we face death all day long; we are considered as sheep to be slaughtered." No, in all these things we are more than conquerors through Him who loved us. For I am convinced that neither death nor life, neither angels nor demons, neither the present nor the future, nor any powers, neither height nor depth, nor anything else in all creation, will be able to separate us from the love of God that is in Christ Jesus our Lord" Romans 8:35-39 NIV.

Hollace and Charlotte, I salute you. God has made you more than conquerors. God's got this.

The Valley of the Shadow of Death

The shadow of the boy's coffin fell upon Jesus' feet. He stepped up. He felt her pain in the pit of His stomach and it moved Him toward her sorrow. "Don't cry," Jesus whispered to her, and He wiped away her tear. He would walk with her through the valley of the shadow of death and lead her out to the green pastures of the living.

"What an absurd thing to request," Sarah thought. Her tears had flowed unabated since the moment her son had breathed his last breath. They came despite her will to be strong. The sorrow overwhelmed her and knocked her to her knees when she least expected it. She only wished she could stop crying. Then she saw this strange Rabbi walk to her son's open casket.

Jesus halted the procession when He touched the coffin. He looked the angel of death in the face and spoke to the boy, "Young man, I say to you get up!" The only Son of God stood confidently while the only son of the widow rose talking. The living held their breath while the dead boy sat up.

Jesus carried him back to his mother. It was a mother and child reunion and they embraced; Jesus smiled; the crowd applauded, and mourning was turned into dancing.

Waypoints to your destination:

What is your sorrow today?

Do you think your situation is too far out of God's reach?

What was the widow's circumstance?

What did the centurion do that made Jesus marvel?

"Lord, give me the faith of the centurion. Humbly I come. Give me faith Lord, and with my faith and by Your power, may I move mountains."

Sweet Hour of Prayer

Day Forty

"And it came to pass, that as He was praying in a certain place, when He ceased, one of His disciples said unto Him, Lord, teach us to pray, as John also taught his disciples" Luke 11:1 KJV.

And He said unto them, when you pray, say,
"Our Father which art in heaven,
Hallowed be thy name.
Thy kingdom come.
Thy will be done in earth as it is in heaven.
Give us this day our daily bread.
And forgive us our debts as we forgive our debtors.
And lead us not into temptation
but deliver us from evil:
For thine is the kingdom and the power,
and the glory forever.
Amen."
Matthew 6:9-13 KJV.

Friend, can you call God, "Our Father?" It's the one name He desires to hear more than any other. He wants you to become His child through His Only Begotten Son, Jesus our Christ. We don't need vain repetitions as we call on the Lord. One name is all we need. "Father." In Aramaic it is Abba.

It means Papa. He alone is our provider. God alone forgives and God alone delivers us from evil.

I pray these last forty days have led you into an intimate relationship with Jesus, Son of God, Son of Man. He came from heaven to earth to blaze a trail back to the One who created you. I hope the places and the people we met throughout this book have drawn you into His inner circle. Did you see your story told through some of their stories? I did. I have been like Nicodemus seeking Jesus with all my questions. I identify with Simon Peter who just can't stop talking. Often I recognized people I wanted to become. I want to be Andrew who became the first missionary. He brought His brother Simon to Jesus. Again, here I am. I could go on and on. I am many of the people we met on our journey.

At the end of the quest though, I need to pause, quiet myself and just ask, "Jesus, teach me to pray."

Waypoints to your destination:

Take some time alone today.

Go to a certain quiet place and just begin.

"Our Father…"

Epilogue

"The Road goes ever on and on down from the door where it began. Now far ahead the Road has gone, and I must follow, if I can, pursuing it with eager feet, until it joins some larger way." J. R. R. Tolkien

They were the first Jesus called. He had written a different story for each of them. He became the center of their days. They had no idea what awaited them at every village they visited. He sent them out two by two and called them His apostles. They were to be Jesus' ambassadors. He gave them His authority and power over unclean spirits.

"They drove out many demons and anointed many sick people with oil and healed them" Mark 6:13 NIV.

"The apostles gathered around Jesus and reported to Him all that they had done and taught. He said to them, "Come away by yourselves to a remote place and rest for a while" Mark 6:30-31 HCSB.

The seclusion Jesus called them to would bring them back to ground zero. It was not what they had done, but what He had done through them. It was just another lesson in humility, and they needed to be quieted from the adrenaline rush they had just experienced.

We read their stories from our side of history, but from their side of His Story their ordinary became extraordinary. They went to sleep with wow and wonder written across their memories because they had seen water changed to wine, lepers healed, and demons fled at His word. Their very lives were changed for the better when Jesus intersected their day. The disciples wrote a story worth telling and their story has become our legacy. We can relate to their stories of redemption and brokenness. Their Hero is our Hero also.

Everyone yearns to become part of a narrative of an epic adventure. We have an innate desire to live a life worth living. The story of our lives was written by an adventurous Storyteller. God planted an incredible journey in every human heart. He has wired us to be a part of His Story. It is a voyage to Eternity filled with carnivals of joy and pain. He wrote the script and built the sets. He is the author and perfector of our faith. God is the director and producer of our film and He has written in us a story worth telling.

This is an amazing race God created us for. It is filled with surprises, laughter, tears, hurts, fears, and victories. You may bleed a little along the way and the voyage may make you seasick. At times the scenery surrounding you will be majestic mountaintops, or tranquil turquoise seas. You may want to pause a while to give praise. That's good. It is what we are called to do, and yet the journey will continue.

We can't get stuck in the smaller stories of our lives. The journey toward Eternity is just that, a journey. It is a marathon and not a sprint. There is a final destination, a final act to our play. God has it all written out.

"Lord, I know that people's lives are not their own; it is not for them to direct their steps" Jeremiah 10:23 NIV.

The chapter we currently find ourselves in may consume us, obscuring the Creator's path, but God knows the way out of our maze. He is the Voice of our eternal GPS. He has plotted every highway and byway of our lives. We just need to plug into His directions. Just as Jesus called each of His disciples, He calls us to follow His journey. He asks us to start at our current location. We may be asked to retrace our steps. Rocks and thorns may trip us up, but Jesus will always be at our side leading us to eternity. We need only to trust His directions. An everlasting kingdom awaits us.

The disciple's journey had just begun. After Jesus' ascension into heaven and having received the promised Holy Spirit, they would begin a movement called, "The Way," but from the moment Jesus called their name day in and day out they would follow Jesus "On The Way" to His final destination. Oh, the things they would see. Oh, the things they would experience. And, oh, the heartache they would feel when they followed Him up a hill called Golgotha. In my next book, "Up the Hill" we will climb with Jesus as He resolutely marches up calvary's hill. What seemed like certain defeat became His victor crown. "Up the hill," is coming in the spring of 2020.

Next time you text, "On the way," remember to live big, follow Jesus, and tell a story worth telling!

L'Chaim! To life everyone

Book One

Through Their Eyes

Here is what people are saying about, "Through Their Eyes."

"Through Their Eyes is a perfect history lesson for the Christmas season. We loved using it as a family devotional and teaching our kids the true meaning of Christmas. I highly recommend it!"
Nikki Pressnall

"I love how the book brought the first Christmas people to life for me. The book shed a whole new light on their personalities. I experienced Christmas in a way that gave me a truer meaning to this Holy time."
Kevin Jones

Book Three

With the Love of God

"I love you with the love of God," I say to Asher and Lucas and Zeke and Jax as I leave them. I always walk away wondering, "Is that a correct statement?" Can any human love another human with the endless, faithful, and unconditional love of our Heavenly Father? It is a love so great that caused Him to send His One and Only Son into our world to die a horrible death just so we can be restored to our Holy God. Step with me into the days when Jesus walked the earth and showed mankind just how much their Creator loved them. Abide with me for forty days in His indescribable love.

The book "With the love of God" we will experience again the gentle touch of a Savior as He reaches out to the lepers, the woman with evil spirits, and the outcasts. "With the Love of God - 40 days of abiding in God's love," is the next book of my 40 day series and will be released 2019.

CPSIA information can be obtained
at www.ICGtesting.com
Printed in the USA
FFOW02n2114280318
46065351-47081FF